WHAT PEOPLE ARE SAYING ABOUT
Reconcilable Differences

This book brings together two qualities that are often sadly separated in evangelical discourse on this subject—conviction and charity. Nancy and Alice demonstrate that it is possible to be tough-minded without being narrow-minded.

—DR. TIMOTHY GEORGE
DEAN, BEESON DIVINITY SCHOOL, SAMFORD UNIVERSITY AND
EXECUTIVE EDITOR OF *CHRISTIANITY TODAY*

With sparkling prose and lively anecdotes, Reconcilable Differences will stretch your faith as well as affirm it.

—BEVERLY LEWIS
NEW YORK TIMES BEST-SELLING AUTHOR OF
THE PREACHER'S DAUGHTER

In a church more often known for our divisions than by our love for one another, Nancy and Alice remind us once again that among the followers of Jesus love bridges the greatest divides.

—CAROLYN CUSTIS JAMES
AUTHOR OF *WHEN LIFE AND BELIEFS COLLIDE* AND *LOST WOMEN OF THE BIBLE* AND PRESIDENT, WHITBY FORUM

What a refreshing gift Nancy and Alice have given us as we are invited into our own process of contending with Scripture, culture, history, and most primarily, love.

—JAN MEYERS
AUTHOR OF *THE ALLURE OF HOPE* AND *LISTENING TO LOVE*

For two Christian women of such differing opinions to write a book together on such a volatile subject is for them to invite the rest of us—every person in the church—to show the same love toward each other.

—SARAH SUMNER
AUTHOR OF MEN AND WOMEN IN THE CHURCH AND PROFESSOR OF THEOLOGY AND MINISTRY, AZUSA PACIFIC UNIVERSITY

Reconcilable Differences *is a powerful demonstration of the strength and tenacity of love! Nancy and Alice share their different opinions honestly with passion and clarity, yet without compromise. In spite of their different views, they continue to choose friendship. This is a beautiful demonstration of Paul's words in 1 Corinthians 13: "If I know all mysteries and have all knowledge ... but do not have love, I am nothing."*

—MARGIE BYINGTON
MA, PASTORAL COUNSELING

I know that Reconcilable Differences *is a book that my complementarian friends and I will read together as I begin seminary and the ordination process. After reading this book I am better able to understand my girlfriends who have different opinions—and love them even more.*

—SARA RANDALL
SEMINARY STUDENT

Nancy Parker Brummett *and* Alice Scott-Ferguson

Reconcilable
Differences

Two Friends Debate
God's Role *for* Women

TREE OF LIFE
MINISTRIES — JOHN 10:10
210 N. 21st Street Unit D
Purcellville, VA 20132
703-554-3595
www.tolministries.org

LIFE JOURNEY®
Bringing Home the Message for Life

COOK COMMUNICATIONS MINISTRIES
Colorado Springs, Colorado • Paris, Ontario
KINGSWAY COMMUNICATIONS LTD
Eastbourne, England

Life Journey® is an imprint of
Cook Communications Ministries, Colorado Springs, CO 80918
Cook Communications, Paris, Ontario
Kingsway Communications, Eastbourne, England

RECONCILABLE DIFFERENCES
© 2006 by Nancy Parker Brummett & Alice Scott-Ferguson

All rights reserved. No part of this book may be reproduced without written permission, except for brief quotations in books and critical reviews. For information, write Cook Communications Ministries, 4050 Lee Vance View, Colorado Springs, CO 80918.

The Web addresses (URLs) recommended throughout this book are solely offered as a resource to the reader. The citation of these Web sites does not in any way imply an endorsement on the part of the author or the publisher, nor does the author or publisher vouch for their content for the life of this book.

Cover Design: Zoë Tennesen-Eck Design
Cover Photo Credit: ©JupiterImages

First Printing, 2006
Printed in the United States of America

1 2 3 4 5 6 7 8 9 10 Printing/Year 11 10 09 08 07 06

All scripture quotations, unless otherwise noted, are taken from the *Holy Bible, New International Version*®. *NIV*®. Copyright © 1973, 1978, 1984 by International Bible Society. Used by permission of Zondervan. All rights reserved. Scripture quotations marked AB are taken from *The Amplified Bible*. Copyright © 1954, 1958, 1962, 1964, 1965, 1987 by The Lockman Foundation. Used by permission; and MSG are taken from THE MESSAGE. Copyright © by Eugene H. Peterson 1993, 1994, 1995, 1996, 2000, 2001, 2002. Used by permission of NavPress Publishing Group. Italics in Scripture have been placed by the authors for emphasis.

ISBN-13: 978-0-7814-4358-6
ISBN-10: 0-7814-4358-X

LCCN: 2006927281

*To our two Jims
with love and gratitude
for their steadfast support*

*There is one body and one Spirit—
just as you were called to one hope when you were called—
one Lord, one faith, one baptism;
one God and Father of all,
who is over all and through all and in all.*

—Ephesians 4:4–6

Contents

Acknowledgments 9
Introduction 11
Prologue 13
    Nancy's Spiritual Journey 13
    Alice's Spiritual Journey 22

1. **Wondering Who We Are: The Essential Woman** .. 29
       What is a woman's true identity? 29
       Is she equal to her male counterpart? 36
       What are our gender roles? 45

2. **Saying I Do: The Design of a Wife** 55
       Who or what is a wife? 55
       Must a wife submit to her husband? 63
       Should a wife support headship? 77

3. **Giving for a Lifetime: Motherhood** 89
       To be or not to be? 89
       Is motherhood necessary for fulfillment? 97
       What does a "good mother" look like? 103

4. **Finding Our Niche: The Working Woman** 113
   When is work productive and satisfying? 113
   Should a woman work outside the home? 120
   Can we afford our choices? 130

5. **Following Our Calling: The Ministry of a Woman** . . 139
   What is a woman's role inside the church? 139
   How does she minister outside the church? 154
   What does God expect? 159

6. **Confronting Hard Questions: Challenging Issues** . . 163
   Can a Christian be a feminist? 163
   How does a Christian handle divorce? 170
   Does the single woman need male covering? 179
   Can a lesbian be a Christian? 185

7. **Leaving Our Hearts Behind: A Lasting Legacy** . . . 193
   How can we distinguish freedom from oppression? . . 193
   How can older women best mentor younger ones? . . 198
   What will we leave our daughters and granddaughters? . . 207

8. **Loving One Another Anyway: Unity in Christ** . . . 219
   What is our common ground? 219
   How do we become one despite our differences? 224
   Is there a place at Jesus' table for every woman? . . . 230

Epilogue 235

Readers' Guide 241

Notes 247

Recommended Reading List 251

About Nancy 254

About Alice 255

Acknowledgments

WE OWE A debt of gratitude to so many people who have influenced our lives and, in so doing, become a part of the thoughts and beliefs we've shared in this book. Relatives, teachers, pastors—all have left imprints on our souls and shaped our opinions.

From the very beginning of this journey we were surrounded by faithful friends and other excellent women who were willing to open their hearts to us and give us the privilege of sharing in their lives. From those who gathered to discuss topics to those who read and commented on parts of the manuscript, we thank you so much.

Above all, we thank the Lord for his relentless reassurance that this collaboration was his idea. In his perfect time this book is now in your hands.

To him be the glory.

Introduction

THEY WILL KNOW we are Christians by our love. But what happens when Christians disagree? Can we still model love to the world, and find it in our hearts to love one another? Everyone knows how hard that is. Especially the two of us.

We became friends several years ago when we were part of the same writers' critique group. As our respect for one another's work was growing, so was our friendship. Alice was drawn to Nancy's poise, polish, and sonorous Southern accent. Nancy was drawn to Alice's warmth, her mastery of the English language, and her lilting Scottish brogue.

In the beginning, we knew nothing of each other's views on women's roles. But that soon changed. Our strong opinions couldn't be hidden for long. Alice embraces an egalitarian line of thought, advocating the removal of inequalities among all people, while Nancy takes a more complementarian approach, espousing that God created men and women as equals with different gender-defined roles. We still laugh over the day Alice called Nancy from the cell phone in her car to say, "I'm listening to some of your complementarian tapes, and I've nearly driven off the road. How can you believe this stuff?" Still, we realized the Lord had purposely brought us together as colleagues, friends, and sisters in the faith.

Our overriding intent in writing this book is to bring unity born out of love as we equip you to make your own decisions about the roles of the Christian woman. Love and respect are certainly needed in the ongoing discussion about these roles—a love and respect that we, although of polarized positions, continue to discover and enjoy as we "make every effort to keep the unity of the Spirit through the bond of peace" (Eph. 4:3).

Whenever a climate of criticism, intolerance, and dissension prevails in the church, love is always the first casualty. No matter how vital certain doctrines are—and we believe that gender issues are extremely important—contending for any truth at the expense of love is detrimental to the Christian faith.

If you are a woman who hasn't fully embraced the Christian life because you don't know where you stand on these issues, it is our prayer that your exposure to our very different life journeys will show you there is a place at the Lord's Table for every woman—a place saved just for you. If you have been a believer for years but grappled with issues like submission and male headship, we hope our heartfelt responses to the questions raised will help you clarify your own thoughts and beliefs. In addition to the careful research we have done, our credentials are a great love for our God, diligent devotion to the Scriptures, and many years of combined life experience.

Regardless of where you are on your journey, we trust that the unity in Christ we both know and enjoy will be yours as well. It is our prayer that the words of this book will reflect the plea of Saint Augustine who wrote, "In essentials, unity, in nonessentials liberty, and in all things, love."

Prologue

Life's a voyage that's homeward bound.
—Herman Melville

Nancy's Spiritual Journey

I CLEARLY REMEMBER the day I joined a Presbyterian church in Knoxville, Tennessee. I can still feel the crisp, starched skirt of the white dress I wore. I remember the cool wood of the pew underneath me, the smell of the flowers on the altar, and the butterflies in my stomach as I walked to the front of the church to profess my faith. I'll never forget my first taste of wine as the sacraments were passed, and how it burned all the way down, seeming to fill me with the warmth of the Holy Spirit.

But my spiritual journey began years before that day. My sisters and I were in Sunday school and church every Sunday. We always sat in the same pew and usually giggled during the hymns. My dad nodded off at just about the same time in the sermon each week. My mother always thanked "the good Lord" for all things in our lives and she still does. I was raised in a Christian home.

As an adult I attended church too, serving faithfully on committees, singing in the choir, taking part in services, etc. But the churches I belonged to were not churches that openly talked about a personal relationship with Jesus Christ and the need to make him both Lord and Savior of our lives.

Did I believe in God the Father Almighty, the Creator of the universe? Certainly. Did I believe in Jesus Christ, his only Son who died for my sins? Absolutely. Had I surrendered my life to him and asked him to rule over every part of it? Not really.

But the Lord has a way of seeking his own. Through the events and tragedies of my life, he brought me closer to him. As is so common, it wasn't until I found out the hard way that I couldn't control everything that I relinquished control to him.

In my adolescence and early adulthood I was blessed with what some would consider a charmed life. I excelled in high school and at the University of Tennessee, accumulating a long list of activities and honors along the way. It was at UT that I met my first husband, and I worked hard to graduate early so we could get married and set off on a military career that took us to Germany and gave a young Tennessee girl a chance to see the world.

What began as a storybook college romance ended in the tragedy of divorce thirteen years later. I'm still not completely sure what happened to my first marriage. My husband was a military officer. There was a war in Vietnam. We moved a lot. And Satan quite simply found a playground inside a marriage that wasn't adequately protected by a hedge of prayer, a marriage containing two people intent on meeting their own personal needs, a marriage where Christ was an outsider, not an equal partner.

Caught up in this tragedy were two little boys. They were not quite eight and eleven the summer we summoned them

Prologue

into the living room and told them that their father would be moving on to his next duty station without us. The little one, Tim, cried immediately, hugging us both and telling us he loved us very much. The older one, Rob, sat silently ... no tears, no comments. Only hours later did he say, "What I want doesn't matter. You're going to do what you're going to do no matter what I say, so why should I say anything?" And the anger and hurt inside him began to build.

The following summer, having survived the first of seven years I would spend as a single mom, I took the boys back to Knoxville to visit my family. I had the privilege of being able to return to the same house my sisters and I grew up in, the same house I came home to as a newborn. I am the middle of three girls, and it was in that house that we played with our dolls under the dining room table and slid down the banister. We rode our bikes in the same driveway where we later smooched with our boyfriends until my dad flicked the porch light on and off to tell us it was time to come in. I went home in a very real sense.

In this memory-rich context, my children's father picked them up to take them to New Jersey for six weeks. I still remember the emptiness I felt as I watched them drive down the driveway. Adding to my pain was the fear that Rob might decide to stay with his dad and go to school in New Jersey, and I might not ever really have him home again.

It was a typical hot, muggy June day in Tennessee when they left. My answer to the pain I was experiencing was to put on my jogging clothes and tell my mom I was going over to my old high school to jog around the track. Just being in that setting again was extremely emotional for me. It reminded me of cheerleading at football games, my high school friends and activities, and of a time in my life when I still believed all my dreams would come true.

As I jogged around the track, uncontrollable tears mingled with the drops of sweat running down my face. I kept running, but I couldn't stop crying. Finally, I dropped to my knees, lifted my face to the sky, and sobbed. "Lord, I can't do this anymore. I can't control what's happening, and even if I could, I don't know the right answers. I've made such a mess of things on my own. Please help me."

If there was one defining moment in my life when I surrendered completely to him, it was that moment. From then on, I became more than a Sunday Christian. The letting-go process took time, and I still find myself clinging to certain things too tightly, but since I asked for his help, I've had the assurance of the Holy Spirit reminding me that my life is in more capable hands than my own. The more I allow Jesus to be Lord of my life in every way, the better I know him. The better I know him, the more I desire his simple, yet gloriously satisfying way of living.

About two weeks after I got back to Colorado from sending the boys off, I got a letter from Rob, addressed in his twelve-year-old handwriting. I nervously opened it walking up the driveway from the mailbox. "Dear Mom," it said. "I have decided I want to go to school in Colorado, if that's OK with you. I miss you. See you soon. Love, Rob." I was elated, but I'll never know if Rob would have been better off in New Jersey—because for the next five years, Satan, the Lord, and I battled for his soul as he went through what can only be described as a tortuous adolescence.

During those years I was also trying to regain my self-esteem through my job as a writer and manager, community activities, and a dating life I wish I could do all over again. Although I was learning more about the Lord all the time, I was far from living the Christian life. Yet I told myself I put my family first as much as possible.

In the midst of all this, the Lord in his wisdom and mercy sent a wonderful Christian man into my life. Jim and I began dating in 1985. He endured many of the parenting challenges with me, and then helped me realize in 1987, when Rob finally hit bottom, that I had become totally codependent. He pointed out that my personal happiness and self-esteem were directly connected to Rob's, and my guilt and concern for Rob were consuming my life. Moreover, my persistent rescuing of Rob was going to kill him.

The Lord told me the same thing. One night I cried myself to sleep over what to do next. (Not an uncommon thing for a single mom to do.) When I awoke, I had the feeling the Lord was shaking me, then that he was throwing me into a chair in the corner of my bedroom. "Please let go of that boy!" he said sternly. "I can't do a thing with him if you won't let go."

I did let go, and the consequences were not all good. Yet the Lord was faithful, and used the path he had chosen, not the one I thought best, to bring my son into full, productive adulthood. Today he's a college graduate, a business owner, and a loving Christian husband and father. He also plays his guitar for the worship team at his small-town church each week and often gives the message. God does good work when we give him control.

Just as Rob grew in the Lord after I let go of him, I grew too. The sanctification process, the lifelong process Christians go through as they become more and more like Jesus, began in me the moment I surrendered my life to the Lord on that muggy day in Tennessee. When I returned to work that summer, a friend who had heard about my divorce dropped a piece of paper on my desk with a Scripture verse on it. It was Jeremiah 29:11: "'For I know the plans I have for you,' declares the LORD, 'plans to prosper you and not to harm you, plans to give you hope and a future.'" It was the Lord working through her, for when I talked to her I found out there was a group of women at work meeting weekly in a Bible study. I began meeting with them and learning what it meant to live all day every day with Jesus Christ.

My first Bible study was followed by many more, and Jim and I began going to a very strong, evangelical, nondenominational church where we both grew under the solid teaching we received. We dated for three years before we were brave enough to merge teenagers, as he had two girls just a bit older than each of my two boys. We became the Brummett Bunch in July of 1988. Since both of us were divorced, we knew this marriage would work only if we put Christ in the center of it.

Once again, the Lord set about to free me, this time from the stubborn independence I had developed as a single woman, by giving me the beautiful interdependence of a marriage in Christ. Day by day, it became easier for me to submit to my husband as he endeavored to love me as Christ loves the church, and I began to understand what God intended when he created marriage. I also knew, for the first time, the blessed joy of having a strong spiritual man as my leader and protector.

Yet the Lord wasn't finished freeing me yet. In 1994, for no apparent reason, I felt myself weighed down with guilt from my past. All of the rationalizations I had relied on for twelve years in order to deal with my divorce were stripped away from me, and I felt the weight of my sin in a physical way. I went to work and home again, and went through all the activities of every day, fighting back tears. Every sin I had ever committed, small or huge, covert or overt, seemed to be replaying constantly on the VCR in my head.

I talked to Jim and he held me as I cried late into the night. I prayed and I studied the Word. I went home to Tennessee and went on a long walk with my younger sister, who is also a believer. "Why now?" I asked her. "Why am I feeling so convicted now when I'm so happily married and the boys are doing so well?"

"Because the Lord knew you couldn't handle it earlier," was her simple, sage reply.

Prologue

In Psalm 32:4–5, David writes: "For day and night your hand was heavy upon me; my strength was sapped as in the heat of summer. Then I acknowledged my sin to you and did not cover up my iniquity. I said, 'I will confess my transgressions to the LORD'—and you forgave the guilt of my sin." Not just his sin, but even the guilt of his sin. My experience was much like David's.

I thought I had confessed my sins years before, but I had never dared to look at them as nakedly as the Lord forced me to do now. This time when I asked his forgiveness, it was with a totally contrite heart, and he heard me. Again he came to me as in a dream or a vision. I saw Jesus holding a pair of scissors. It was like a ribbon-cutting, and a wide pink ribbon was stretched in front of him. He looked at me and said, "OK, now I'm going to cut this, and all the sin that has held you captive will be gone forever." The weight immediately left my shoulders, and I knew I never had to replay the videos again.

You see, I had intellectually accepted the message of salvation, but I didn't feel forgiven in my heart until I went through this period of heavy conviction. That the Lord loved me enough to put me through it touched me as nothing else could. I felt freer than I had ever felt in my life. Free to be whatever he wanted me to be ... but what?

At the same time the Lord was showing me spiritual truth, he was helping me clarify the roles I was intended to play. I began to feel him calling me away from my corporate management position and frenetic lifestyle. I didn't know why he filled my heart with a desire to quit my job and go home to an empty nest, populated only by two cats who really didn't want me around disturbing their afternoon naps, but he did. When Jim and I prayed about my quitting my job we seemed to hear the message, "not yet." But when my company offered a voluntary severance package to all employees, it was as if the Lord said to me, "OK, now. Go home." I did.

At first, it felt really strange, but I loved being at home during the day. I loved seeing the sunlight coming through the windows. I began noticing birds again. I didn't know there was a biblical reason for what I was doing at the time (later I learned it came from my desire to be mistress of my domain), but I went into a frenzy, organizing all our closets and cupboards. I even labeled the leftover paint cans so we'd know which paint was used in each room.

I also knew I wanted to replace my "to do" list with a "to be" list. I concentrated on being a writer, on being a grandmother, on being a wife and a woman as never before. A major influence in helping me clearly see what I believe to be the truth about God's plan for women was the *Five Aspects of Woman* Bible study written by Barbara Mouser. The study confirmed what I knew in my heart. It clearly pointed out why I had suffered from past choices, and how the Lord had been revealing his truth to me all along.

God was teaching me so much, and I became overwhelmed with the desire to spare my two stepdaughters, both married, my two daughters-in-law, and my precious granddaughters all the pain and heartache I had known as a product of the women's movement throughout the '70s and '80s. It's a lie that women can "have it all" at the same time. It's a lie that willing submission equals oppression. I wanted them to know these things.

When I think of my growing up years I see that there was more of a spiritual atmosphere in our home than I realized. It wasn't until after my dad died suddenly of a heart attack in 1986 that I came to fully understand the relationship he and my mother shared. What I had misread as his dominance of her was really her active choice to submit to his leadership in our home. I understood, too late to save my first marriage, that she was content and free in her choice, and that the role she played in her marriage had made it possible for my sisters and I to have the stable family life that we enjoyed.

Jim and I pray daily for our children's marriages because we know how devious Satan can be in his plan to destroy marriages and families. I've tried to pass along what I've learned to my daughters-in-law, stepdaughters, and granddaughters through letters to them and the books I have written. Although I realize they'll have to make their own mistakes, and the Lord will reveal his truth to them in his way and in his own time, I want them to know what he has taught me. Most of all, I want them to see how he has freed me to become the woman he wants me to be ... and that he'll do the same for them.

The study of God's Word has also enriched my marriage, which grows stronger with each passing day. If you asked my husband what is best about my working at home as a freelancer, he'd say, "that we get to have real baked potatoes instead of ones cooked in the microwave." Beyond that, he's just so happy to have a "real wife." To have my loyalty and my attention, two things he always had to share with my career before.

God has honored our decision by blessing my husband's business beyond what we could ever imagine. He has also brought many writing opportunities my way so that our income is almost the same as it was when I was working full-time.

I want the women in our family, and as many women as I can reach through my writing and speaking, to see what happens when you get out of your husband's way and let him be the provider and leader God asks him to be. It works. I want to share with them the freedom that comes from obeying the Lord and walking in his ways. I wish I had been able to accept his truth into my heart fully at a younger age, but I don't question his timing. Rather, I am eternally grateful to the Lord for showing me how he has worked through the years to make me a free woman in Jesus Christ. From the pain of divorce and the heartbreak of a prodigal son, God has brought me to a place of peace and balance and then added the blessing of grandchildren. We stand in awe of his ability to exchange "beauty for ashes" in our blended family and of the pouring out of his grace and mercy.

I suppose it is the sum composite of all the experiences of my life, and the knowledge of how God was working in and through them to work all things together for my good, that makes me the complementarian I am today.

In my first marriage I bought into many of the lies of the women's movement and the marriage ended disastrously. In my second marriage, I've learned to seek God's wisdom through his Word and to go to him with all my longings, all my desires. To discover that there is freedom in submission is transforming—and liberating. I know I am equally valued and equally loved by God, but through the events of my life and God's faithfulness to all generations, he has shown me the better way. He continues to direct my steps, and I look forward to serving him by becoming more of the woman he created me to be with each passing day.

> *But one thing I do: Forgetting what is behind*
> *and straining toward what is ahead, I press on*
> *toward the goal to win the prize for which*
> *God has called me heavenward in Christ Jesus.*
>
> —PHILIPPIANS 3:13–14

ALICE'S SPIRITUAL JOURNEY

THE NOISY TV program was simply part of the background bustle of the morning, the squeals of exuberant grandchildren almost obliterating the chatter of the show. Then, as I glanced over at the screen, I paused. The elderly gentleman hosting the game show had snowy white hair and was surrounded by a bevy of beautiful young women. As I switched off, I was forcibly struck with the statement that such a combination made. I could never recall seeing an elderly gray-haired lady on "any time" TV attended by a group of buffed young men. I knew very well that the answer lay in the different societal standards for women and men. As this older woman went on her way that morning, I reflected on my worldview and why I was so aware of the disparities between the genders—so grieved at the inequities, and so outraged at the double standards.

The immense, all-encompassing love of God is what has motivated me to collaborate in the writing of this book. That love causes me to embrace all of the body of Christ, no matter how their persuasions may differ from mine. Over the years, I have come to see that love is the only element that will outlive every doctrine, and that no persuasion or conviction is worth risking its loss—not even gender equality. We quite forget that Paul's famous love chapter (1 Cor. 13) is the love imperative that it is, so we settle for its soft sounds at wedding ceremonies. The unequivocal statement that if we have not love we have nothing goes largely unheeded as we quibble over the lesser issues. However, that same love persuades me that God would never see women and men as anything but totally equal. I still hold that truth to be self-evident, only hold it framed in love, not dissension.

My emancipated journey began in the farthest outpost of the United Kingdom: an archipelago of approximately one hundred islands called the Shetlands. This windswept piece of real estate lies 250 miles northeast of the nearest Scottish mainland and is situated equidistant from Norway. In the rural area, the occupation of the islanders was traditionally divided between the land and the sea. The work was hard and bred endurance and faith. My father, like most of the men of the community where I grew up, spent many months of the year at sea. The smallholdings (known as crofts) of these farmers and fishermen could not adequately sustain their families so they often made a second career at sea in order to supplement the family income. They may have enlisted in the merchant navy for a time or embarked on extended whaling trips to the Antarctic. The women, including my mother with me at her side, were left behind to take care of both family and farm work.

Every day my mother would bring in a big bucket of potatoes from the field or the storeroom. These tubers were used for food for both humans and livestock, hence the brimming bucketful. On one occasion I perched myself up beside her with my little knife, eager to get my hands into the loamy-laden lumps and help her prepare the potatoes for the pot. Her welcome was not what I had expected and, although I felt slighted at the time, what she said lodged in my mind because of its far-reaching vision for her little girl. "My little one, your hands were meant for better things than peeling potatoes." No Martha Stewart in the making, I'm afraid! The aspirations that my mother had for me extended far beyond those northern horizons—far away from the land of the midnight sun where that golden orb never sets at the height of summer, and where the aurora borealis light up the long, dark winter skies with their colorful, merry dances.

My father also raised me to see women as strong and unthreatened—capable of doing anything. He treated all women with great respect, affirmed their skills, and saw his daughter as capable of achieving her dreams as his son was his. It never occurred to me that there were doors that were closed to me because of my gender. Many years had to pass before I discovered that being a woman was a hindrance to achievement, particularly in the church. Also, having a father like that made it very easy to see my heavenly Father as a God who loved and valued me equally to my male counterparts. I knew that his opinion of me was wonderful, emancipated, and the horizon of my life was limitless.

My grandmothers left a lasting impression on me too. I remember them as strong, spunky, and kind—women who were devoted to their homes, their families, and their God despite loneliness, hardships, and death. My maternal grandmother buried not only her husband, she also outlived five of her children. Two of them died at the tender ages of eighteen and twenty-two. She is the woman who leaned over and whispered to me in a context long-forgotten, "You can't love anyone else until you love yourself." That, like my mother's potato episode, is what I label a frozen frame in time—words that sowed strong and healthy seeds into the tender, impressionable soil of a young life.

With such a background, it is not surprising that I met and married a man who also advocates freedom and equal rights for women. He continues to be my greatest champion, supporting and encouraging me to claim the high ground of emancipated living. Throughout most of our child-raising years, we were, by choice, in traditional mode. Although I was an adoring mother who stayed at home until my youngest was eleven, I knew that my identity was in neither being a wife nor mother. Nor did I find it in my temporarily laid aside nursing career. My identity lay, and forever lies, in Christ alone.

Support groups for women were rare at that time, and even less available for men. So the onus fell on the woman to facilitate change and enhancement in a marriage. It was implied that a woman's greatest satisfaction and fulfillment was to be found in being a wife and mother and any desire to fulfill one's life beyond that was frowned upon. I remember driving home from a seminar that advocated this, tears streaming down my face, crying out to the Lord, "Why have you put all this passion in my soul, if I have no opportunity to fulfill this calling to teach and preach?" In good time, he would answer the cry of my heart.

In the meantime, motherhood was a joy to me. I never considered it a secondary occupation: only that it was not the sole acme of my achievement. I did not yearn for great status in the corporate world; I did not want to pursue ordination and take a pulpit; I had no interest in joining the armed forces to command a troop of men. I didn't consider homemaking an art beneath my dignity; I didn't want my husband to stay home and take care of the children. I didn't want to lose my femininity. I grieved only at the paradigm that dictated I should not be any of these other things if I wanted to. I intuitively knew that the discrepancy was wrong, that it was not what God intended for his creation—a creation intended to reflect his own image, which is both male and female.

When I resumed my career in nursing, specializing in psychiatric care, I never adopted the obsequious demeanor that was prevalent amongst nurses towards their colleagues, the doctors—even when it was risky not to. When transcribing one psychiatrist's orders to the medical card that gave the staff the dosage of a patient's medication, I transcribed it wrongly due to the doctor's illegible scrawl. I got into trouble from my supervisor for this error and so took what I thought was the obvious next step: I respectfully confronted the offending physician. I suppose that really was a bold move, but the result was a mutual respect between us to the extent that he authored a glowing reference when I later moved on to other employment.

However, nursing wasn't my ideal career. Had there been other, more obvious career options for girls at the juncture of my life when I first made that choice, I might not have found myself gazing at the Georgian facades of the newspaper houses in the city of Edinburgh during my off-duty hours wishing that I was writing bylines rather than bustling with bedpans.

After several years back in the nursing profession, I finally came to a trajectory that started me on a course that would confirm my confidence in God's egalitarian view and of his great plans to answer the cry of my heart. By now, I lived in a small mountain town in Colorado. At the end of one grueling day at work I came home, made a cup of coffee, and collapsed into a patio chair to exhale the stress and to inhale the majesty of the Rocky Mountains. And to talk to my heavenly Father. "Lord, take everything I am through education, experience, personality and use it all for your purposes." Opportunities to teach in women's seminars opened up rapidly and, within a few months of that God-inspired prayer, my husband and I were relocated to England where I founded and directed a ministry to women that blazed the length and breadth of Britain and beyond for the next ten years.

The words of my grandmother now were immortalized as I, under the leadership of the Holy Spirit, spread the message of God's unconditional love for women. The message empowered them to believe that they could do all things through Christ who was in them. The first congregation with which we were divinely connected supplied most of the women who would join me in this mission after they first claimed that freedom for themselves. I received much opposition from certain quarters in the church hierarchy—usually men who used scattered Scripture passages to support their supremacy. It took unassailable confidence in my heavenly Father's assignment to go on. The Holy Spirit fortified me on many occasions as he graciously, gently, and repeatedly affirmed that I was obeying the mandate God had given me. I knew I had to obey God rather than men. I used the erroneous objections to fertilize the soil out of which the abundant and sweet fruit of freedom sprouted.

I wish I had known about Christians for Biblical Equality during those hard years of establishing a women's ministry. It was not until many years later at a writer's conference in New Mexico that author Jan Johnson drew me aside and whispered that I needed to know about CBE. She sat beside me at the breakfast table and detected a "free" spirit who did not conform to expected norms. I wondered at first to what nefarious group she was referring, but now I am indebted to their faithful, diligent, and meticulous study of the Scriptures that has resulted in an abundance of apologetics, books, and papers that champion the cause of egalitarians.

God is utterly faithful and nothing can thwart his purpose for us. Remembering what you loved to do as a child gives clues to the original genius within. During the long winter evenings of my childhood in those far-flung isles (with no television to watch), one of my favorite occupations was to write. I would write girl's adventure stories on whatever scrap paper I could find, mainly the back of calendar pages. There was no Office Max from which to buy a ream of paper and no discarded copies from computers, for they did not exist in my world either. When a neighbor asked me if I was going to write a book when I grew up I replied, quite prophetically as it transpired, "Yes, when I am sixty I will publish a book." My first book came out in the fall of that very year, not by design, but by destiny.

> *For as many of you as were baptized into Christ [into a spiritual union and communion with Christ, the Anointed One, the Messiah] have put on (clothed yourselves with) Christ. There is [now no distinction] neither Jew nor Greek, there is neither slave nor free, there is not male and female; for you are all one in Christ Jesus.*
>
> —GALATIANS 3:27–28 AB

Chapter 1

Wondering Who We Are

The Essential Woman

*There is in every true woman's heart
a spark of heavenly fire.*

—WASHINGTON IRVING

WHAT IS A WOMAN'S TRUE IDENTITY?

"I AM WOMAN, hear me roar/In numbers too big to ignore...." The words of Helen Reddy's famous song that reigned at number one on the Billboard charts in 1972 were a rallying refrain for many women seeking to establish a clear identity in that era. In more recent times, who can forget seeing the moving TV footage of women in Iraq forming long and patient lines waiting to vote for the very first time. We certainly heard them "roar" and in numbers way too many to ignore. A woman's identity is certainly classified and defined when

ALICE

she finally finds her voice—whether in a repressive regime, in a rocky relationship, or in a career change. However, regardless of place, time, or circumstance, there is something more to the identity of a woman.

Beyond any other designation, a woman is an essential, integral part of the expression of God. She is made in the image of her Creator. The Bible declares that we were made in his image, male and female (Gen. 1:26–27). Man reflects the masculine side of God and woman reflects the feminine component of our Creator. God made us what he is—equally male and female. That is the image of oneness that he wants to show the world.

When men and women are at odds, trying to prove superiority (such as which gender is smarter in the sciences) or going it alone (as reflected in the growing notion that women do not need a father other than to implant the seed), we are living far beneath the original intent. When we insist on narrowly defining a woman according to her biology, her physical uniqueness, and feminine traits, we have failed to see the bigger picture. When religion conveys that one part of the Godhead is bigger, better, or more dominant than the other, we represent a distorted and lopsided representation of the One whose image we bear.

The first male and female humans each enjoyed secure mutual identities before the fall. When sin entered the system that all changed. Renowned worldwide missionary La Donna Osborn sums up and supports this opinion so very well. "In the fall, we saw dignity perverted into shame, purpose interrupted and absolutely shattered because of fear, and equality destroyed. Separation came to describe the human family. Separation resulted in men ruling women, the strong ruling the weak, the rich ruling the poor. Everything about fallen humanity depicts that separation."[†, 1]

The fall maligned our identities, but God's remedy for the rift was already in place in the far reaches of eternity past (Rev. 13:8). In the fullness of time that plan became visible to humankind and we witnessed the heart of God that gave us healing hope: one Person died to take on the sin that the first humans caused (Rom. 5:15). This action abrogated the alienating effects of the fall. The result was personal reconciliation with our Creator, the breaking down of the wall of enmity and division between men and women, and an entire new identity—a grand slam of justice and reconciliation.

The apostle Paul declared that the divisions between Jew and Greek, slave and free, male and female were rendered null and void (Gal. 3:28). In fact, redeemed people are designated an entirely new status, that of a new creation (2 Cor. 5:17).

What is a woman's true identity? Quite simply, she is in Christ.

---

† I encourage the reader to reacquaint herself with the account of the loss and shame that resulted from unilateral activity in the garden as recorded in the third chapter of Genesis.

IMAGINE A BEAUTIFUL, pristine garden lush with every kind of tree and plant. Sparkling waters run in rivers through this perfect sanctuary where Adam, recently created by God in the image of God, sets about his work of naming all the animals. From aardvark to zebra he names them, but as he does, he realizes that unlike the animals, he doesn't have a mate. He doesn't have another living creature who is like him, created in the image of God. He has no one with whom he can talk, or walk through the lush garden, or snuggle with under the stars.

God sees Adam's need. "But for Adam, no suitable helper was found," we read in Genesis 2:20. "So the LORD God caused the man to fall into a deep sleep; and while he was sleeping, he took one of the man's ribs and closed up the place with flesh. Then the LORD God made a woman from the rib he had taken out of the man, and he brought her to the man" (Gen. 2:21–22).

Imagine Adam waking after his surgery at the Master's hand. Through the mist he senses God is approaching again. The task of naming the animals demonstrated that God gave Adam authority on earth. He no doubt wonders what God will ask him to do this time. But then Adam rubs his eyes and sees that God is not alone. With him is the most beautiful creature he has ever seen. Her body is soft where Adam's is hard and curved where his is straight. With serenity on her face and smoothness in her walk, she is perfect femininity. She is woman.

Continuing his task of naming, Adam first names this new creation woman. After the fall, he names her Eve, because she would become the mother of all the living (Gen. 3:20). He takes her into his life and into his heart as the creature God made from him, for him, and brought to him to be his helper and his completer. She was and is the perfect gift, the part of God's handiwork that he saved to be its very crown. For it was not until she was made that God looked over his entire creation and deemed it very good.

Within this amazing creation story is everything we really need to know about who we are as women. But the question I have to ask myself every time I read this is whether the men in our lives today find our presence as welcoming as Adam first found Eve's. When we enter a room, do our husbands' hearts leap at the very sight of us? God would have it be so.

However, you also know the rest of the story. Perfection wasn't to last forever. Evil entered the garden in the form of a serpent who beguiled Eve, opening the door for her and Adam to sin by doing the one thing God asked them not to do. Once Adam and Eve bit into the fruit of the tree of the knowledge of good and evil, they were no longer perfect, nor would their offspring be.

When you continue to read through the Old Testament you understand the extent to which women fell from their perfect, created state. Women and children weren't even counted when a census was taken, and were often considered possessions along with the cattle and the clay pots. Women were considered "unclean" when they were having their menstrual periods. In

Genesis 19:6–8 we are horrified to read of a father, Lot, who, with no apparent qualms, was willing to hand over his virgin daughters to strange men with evil intent. The horrors go on and on.

But that is not the end of the story. The redeemed woman of Christ is free to be all that God created her to be because of his death and resurrection. Rather than take her cues from feminist literature or afternoon talk shows, she can find within the whole counsel of God's Word a complete definition of her redeemed purpose.

Let's focus on what we know for sure. Woman was created from man, for man. Her created purpose was to be his companion, his helper, and his completer. Without her, he couldn't be the man God wanted him to be. Without him, she couldn't fulfill her created purpose. Her body perfectly complemented his and so did her attributes. Together, they became one flesh.

It's also clear that woman had work to do beside her husband. It's no coincidence that man was created from the earth to work the earth and woman was created from the man's side to work by his side. Both man and woman were created in the image of God and both were given the mandate to "Be fruitful and increase in number; fill the earth and subdue it" (Gen. 1:28). She had a domain to manage.

We also see that all human life was to enter the world through woman. Eve gave birth to Cain and Abel and heartbreak resulted, but then Seth and his siblings followed. Ultimately, as God promised when he cursed the serpent at the time of the fall, Jesus came through a woman, Mary, to defeat sin forever. Through the messianic line and up to today we see women fulfilling their roles as life-givers whether through bringing babies into the world or by giving birth to the culture, the beauty, and the quality of life that makes it worth living.

What we see in the creation story is that woman's purpose and her identity are as closely entwined as the vines in the garden of Eden. In Song of Songs 4:15 a woman is compared to "a garden fountain, a well of flowing water." The image brings to mind beauty that is tended and protected so the woman can produce and bring life to the next generation. Yet the feminist movement would strip away this protection for women by convincing them they don't need it—and our culture is damaged in the process.

The types of women are as numerous as the stars in the sky. You need only attend one exercise class to see we come in all shapes and sizes, and with a myriad of gifts. We need to explore verses in both the Old and New Testaments to discover all the God-given roles of women. But it is within the realm of our created design that we find our true identity—and our best opportunity to leave an eternal legacy.

Is She Equal to Her Male Counterpart?

"NOT A MAN in sight." That was my very first thought as I watched the TV footage of the many McArtney sisters from Northern Ireland visiting the White House on St. Patrick's Day 2005. The ardent pursuit of justice for their brother slain by the Irish Republican Army had propelled them across the Atlantic to get the ear of the president. While I admired their guts and determination, I felt sad that, for whatever reason, no men accompanied them.

While the complementarian camp could create a case from this to support its fear that unprotected "petticoats" might render men redundant, the radical feminist faction could seize on it as the epitome of womanpower with no need of its male counterpart. I believe that God's original intent was not for unilateral action, but for mutuality and equality between the sexes.

A constellation of factors contends against this God-ordained equality, and we are often quite unaware of the subtle inequities implied even in everyday parlance. The name of the game of golf, for instance, is reputed to be an acronym for *gentlemen only, ladies forbidden*. While that may come as an amusing surprise, other disparities carry more gravitas. Alvin Schmidt observes in his expansive treatise on how culture shapes society, *Veiled and Silenced*, "The theological enterprise has no choice but to use cultural forms to express its various teachings. No teachings, meanings, or messages can be communicated to human beings apart from given cultural forms and expression."[2] Without a doubt, culture shapes theology and male dominance and female inferiority has deep and tenacious roots in ancient cultures. The church unthinkingly absorbs the mores of the milieu in which we swim.

From those deep and murky waters, women have, over the centuries, been extracted and labeled variously as evil and inferior. Even the seemingly innocuous practice of seating her on the left of the man has significance. The word *left* in Latin is "sinister" which in turn connotes wicked or evil, leaving man on the right—and right. The more serious monikers of witch, harlot, and temptress were common to both the Greek and Roman cultures. Greek men believed that Pandora was the bearer of evil to the world. Even in the biblical account Adam was quick to blame the woman for the evil that befell in the garden.

Schmidt continues in *Veiled and Silenced*, "Where and when the male picture of woman as the one who introduced evil, even death, really began may never be known for certain.... [It] appears to be virtually as old as recorded history, but is also deeply woven into the cultural fabric of many societies."[3]

The lingering legacy of Eve as the originator of evil is well-known in Hebrew history. It persists in its pernicious influence in the liberated church of Christ manifesting in the inequality of the sexes and the misperception that women need to be kept in line, covered, and silenced lest they should continue their nefarious activities and corrupt man, the church, or both. The room or gallery called the *michetza* that separated the women from the men in the synagogue morphed into the less physical, but nonetheless effective, dividing of function and status that we still experience in the church today.

Even in the earliest times the stigma of inferiority was widespread, insidious, and contributed to inequality with her male counterpart. Ancient cultures were unconsciously entrenched in the belief of female inferiority. For example, high mortality rates for women in agrarian societies were interpreted as a sign of weakness rather than as the result of hardship and frequent pregnancies. Women were also rated lower on the scale both intellectually and spiritually. The Old Testament record is replete with instructions, privileges, and positions that apply only to the male.

From these illustrations, it is not difficult to see how disparities between male and female came about. The prevailing thought of the time colors the interpretation and the practice of Christianity, and these accepted practices evolve and change almost as imperceptibly as they developed. A graphic example is evident in the evolved thinking about slavery. The past acceptance of this practice in the United States—which we now consider abhorrent—was endorsed from president to preacher and declared to be a decree of almighty God and sanctioned by the Scriptures.

But glorious good news, the Liberator has come! He turned the law on its head. He came into a world top-heavy with patriarchy, ensnared with impossible and erroneous standards that stretched beyond the parameters of even the law given to Moses, and he turned religious thinking upside down.

From speaking to a Samaritan woman to permitting a bleeding, unclean woman to touch the hem of his garment, Jesus proved that God considered men and women equals; he also made sure that the balance was well and truly redressed.

No more poignant nor definitive a demonstration of shattering unequal status and affirming women is found than in Jesus' attitude towards the patriarchal view of adultery. His response when presented with a woman caught in the act was not to stone her, as the law required, but to forgive her. But he first challenged her accusers to consider their own hearts before they exacted the punishment. One by one they slunk away without a single stone thrown (John 8:1–11).

When we revert to the old covenant, or when we let culture conform us instead of the indwelling life of Christ, or when we substitute tradition for the truth, the outcome is division and disparity in the body of Christ—a community of which we are all equal members.

A WOMAN IS absolutely equal to her male counterpart in every way. She is equally created in the image of God. She is equally saved by the blood of Christ who went to the cross for all, male and female. She is equally valued by her Lord and is coheir, with her husband if married, of the "gracious gift of life" (1 Peter 3:7). But being equal does not mean that she isn't made differently with uniquely feminine contributions to bring to the world and with certain assigned responsibilities to fulfill.

Many women don't understand this distinction. Their desperate desire to "get their fair share" of everything the world offers has fueled the failure of many marriages. I should know; it contributed to the unhappiness in my first marriage.

When things were particularly contentious between us, my first husband told me I was on "the leading edge of the feminist movement" then sweeping our country with social, economic, and political changes. I scoffed at this. After all, I was a stay-at-home mom until both boys were in school, and then I worked only part-time so I could be home when they were. I was a Sunday school teacher and a Cub Scout den mother. Surely I was far from the leading edge of such a forceful, angry movement.

Yet looking back, I realize there was some truth to what he said. It was my heart attitude that was misguided. Ours was not a marriage based on faith—submission wasn't even in my vocabulary. Both of us could have been card-carrying members of the "me generation." My desire was for everything to be 50-50, for everything to be "fair," and to keep my emotional and economic independence apart from my husband. It didn't work.

Through my study of biblical gender issues I have come to understand equality as never before.

Freed from the need to challenge men in order to achieve equality in every arena, I've become comfortable in accepting that men and women are equal in their humanity, but different in their sexuality and gender. I no longer have to struggle with whether the differences are merely cultural, because both the equality and the differences predate all cultures—they are rooted in creation itself, as revealed in Genesis.

And should I ever begin to wonder if God likes men better, all I have to do is look at the way Jesus interacted with women. Setting aside all cultural restraints and customs, Jesus allowed the woman who had been bleeding for twelve years to touch him and be healed. He welcomed the extravagant, loving attention of a woman who poured expensive perfume on his head. He protected the woman caught in adultery, telling her to go and sin no more. He had a special place in his heart for widows and mothers. He went out of his way to encounter a Samaritan woman at the well and reveal to her that he was the Son of God. It was to women that Jesus first spoke after his crucifixion, telling them to go and share the good news that he was alive. Clearly God loves women. He loves men equally, of course, but he created us differently.

In his comprehensive book *Men and Women, Enjoying the Difference*, Dr. Larry Crabb reminds readers that God also clearly loves order, and that we see order in his creation and design for men and women. "There is an essential difference between men and women—a difference that is properly reflected in unique styles of relating both with their worlds and with one another," he writes.[4] "I conclude that there is an order to male-female relationships that is nonreversible because it reflects the differences God built into us," he continues.[5]

What are those differences, beyond the obvious physical ones? There will be exceptions to any generality, but most studies conclude that, in general men are more analytical and nature-focused, women more intuitive and people-focused. Men tend to be objective, focusing on what is, while women tend to be subjective, focusing on how people feel about what is. For example, a man will notice if service is slow in a restaurant, but his wife will notice if the waiter seems depressed. Both viewpoints shed light on the situation, but they are different.

In general, men tend to be risk-takers whereas women are more oriented toward security. Men are the initiators, women the responders. Accordingly, Crabb suggests that men are more prone to engage in activities that have them moving strongly forward in the world whereas women are more likely to engage in activities that invite others into relationship.

Men and women even desire different things. John Eldredge's book *Wild at Heart* struck a chord with men across the nation because he said that, in a man's heart of hearts, he wants a battle to fight, a beauty to rescue, and an adventure to live. The book *Captivating*, written by John and Stasi Eldredge (his wife), beautifully presents the desires and mysteries of a woman's heart: to be protected by a man, to be the beauty he seeks, and to enjoy the adventure with him as she embraces her created role as a captivating daughter of the King.

All these differences are designed by our Creator, not forced upon us by society and culture. Anyone who doubts that just has to look at toddlers at play. Long before they could have been influenced by any gender "shoulds," little girls will display a nurturing, maternal instinct by cradling a stuffed animal if no doll is handy. Likewise, little boys will pick up twigs and say "bang bang." They are innately different.

My husband and I have twice laughed uproariously at regional presentations of Defending the Caveman, the longest running one-man play in Broadway history. The show is so popular because it's based on truth—in this case the more secular anthropological thesis that men are basically hunters while women are gatherers (consider how we shop!). With one hilarious scenario after another these gender differences are pointed out. Yet there's one part of the program where the actor takes a more serious tone. He talks about the man's need to create a safe environment for his woman, a place where she can do all the wonderful, magical things only she can do so well. No one laughs, because his statement strikes a familiar, if long obscured, chord in every male and female heart present. Whether we acknowledge the existence of cave people or not, we know truth when we hear it. Men and women were created differently.

The president of Harvard came under harsh scrutiny in 2005 for intimating that the male and female brains may differ from each other, explaining why males do better in engineering and science fields—and yet many studies prove he is absolutely right. The same studies show that females tend to perform more strongly in verbal and written disciplines, irrespective of cultural influences in school settings or due to having more gray matter in their brains. The male and female IQs may be equal, but their brains are designed differently and perform differently. Why is this so hard to accept? Even the secular world acknowledges that men and women have significant differences.

The most stressed-out women I know are those working night and day to obliterate their natural, God-given feminine tendencies. That's why psychologist John Gray's book, *Men Are from Mars, Women Are from Venus*, enjoyed such a long stint on the bestseller lists and spawned more bestsellers. Women read what he says about gender differences and say, "Now I see why my marriage isn't working." Or, "Now I see why I'm so angry and tired all the time."

"Without the awareness that we are supposed to be different," Dr. Gray writes, "men and women are at odds with each other. We usually become frustrated with the opposite sex because we have forgotten this important truth."[6]

Despite decades of the feminist agenda, women of all faiths who are able to silence the cadence of their equality marches long enough to hear the truth about gender differences also hear the light switch turning on. Dr. Laura Schlessinger

NANCY: has done a great deal through her daily radio program to bring integrity back into our relationships and our homes. When it comes to the feminist goal of creating a gender-neutral world, she says, "I'm sorry, there are differences. In Judaism, women are viewed as being more spiritual than men.... I sorta like the idea that my womanhood and my femininity is exalted, and I am not considered the same as a man. So I don't get the unisex mentality. It has so robbed women of the truth, of the very things which we all seek, which is, we want to be feminine, we want to be respected, we want to mother our children, we want to have healthy relationships. It's not unisex."[7]

We are equal, but we are different. And it is because of our differences that we have been given different roles to play in God's created order.

WHAT ARE OUR GENDER ROLES?

ALICE: OUR ABILITIES AND training have nothing to do with our view of gender issues but everything to do with who we are as individuals. Stereotyping is not a scientific method of the measure of a woman.

"Order-of-creation" theory is presently enjoying a revival as another way to relegate women to certain restrictive roles. Just because the woman was made or taken out of man—formed from the ingredients of Adam—does not put him in a superior position of authority over her any more than the dust of the earth, out of which Adam was made, is superior to or in authority over him. That seems very logical. The order-of-creation argument is an attempt to bind destiny to chronology; such an erroneous exegesis trumps the triumph of the last will and testament of the Lord Jesus Christ who has made a brand-new species in which gender is not a consideration.

Change is challenging. Never more so than when transitioning from the old covenant to the new. Paul writes these revolutionary words: "For man did not come from woman, but woman from man; neither was man created for woman, but woman for man.... *In the Lord,* however, woman is not independent of man, nor is man independent of woman. For as woman came from man, so also man is born of woman. But everything comes from God" (1 Cor. 11:8–9, 11–12). What a magnificent revelation of the difference that being in Christ makes.

Relegation of roles based on gender is restricting and regrettable. It is a worldwide problem, though some disparities are more egregious than others. For the Christian it is in disagreement with the new covenant, and it sets up unnecessary and ungodly competition, hierarchies, and enmity between men and women. The writer Anna Quindlen makes an astute observation about role assignments: "Even Iraq, under our tutelage, has written into its Constitution a guarantee that 25 percent of its legislators will be women. By my count, that means someone owes me 11 senators."[8]

An unknown author wrote, "Humanity's separation from God in pursuit of autonomy introduces a new currency to relationships—conflict." If that autonomy assigns certain personality or emotional gender traits as reason for restrictive roles, it inevitably leads to comparisons that are foolish. To illustrate, hear the words of Carolyn Custis James in her insightful book, *When Life and Beliefs Collide*: "Sympathy and tenderness are not gender traits. They are *Christian* qualities the Holy Spirit generates in both sexes, qualities he intensifies through our theology and calls us to express in our ministry to one another. The fruit of the Spirit, even kindness and gentleness are never divided up by gender. They are attributes of Christ, which all of his followers are called to emulate."[9]

Our gender roles are defined by living to the full the expression of Christ in us—be that vessel female or male. While still on earth Jesus told his disciples that there was much he could not share with them at that time but that when the Holy Spirit came, he would guide us in to all truth (John 16:12–13). He has come as promised, of course. Our teacher is the third person of the Trinity whose knowledge transcends time, cultural mores, and traditional milieu. He represents the unchanging God—now our Father. We know that his bastion of truth will prevail despite the warrens of worldly wisdom that work to undermine it.

Gilbert Bilezikian, that erudite biblical scholar, writes this: "In the course of history, the church has often lost its way. For instance, during a thousand years, the church forgot something as crucial as the way of salvation and replaced it with methods of salvation by works that never worked. The biblical teaching was finally recovered by the Reformers. Likewise, many present-day Christians believe that the church has lost its own definition as community and replaced it with false definitions that reduce it to the status of institution, establishment, and hierarchy.... This challenge provides an incentive to help Christians rediscover for themselves the biblical definition of the church as God's community of oneness."[10]

Our challenge is to do all we can in our own spheres to fulfill the plan of God. Next time you hear reference to *recovering* biblical manhood and womanhood, think about whether you want to recover the role of woman as a chattel, disenfranchised, and one of hundreds of wives to your husband—to say nothing of the concubines he also might own. It is not from the biblical record that we should construct the ideal role relationship, but from the emancipated model of mutuality (Gal. 3:28). Men and women are now equipped to live in mutual honor, celebrating differences as reflections of God—Creator and Redeemer—and as entirely new creations, walking in humble awe at the privilege of showing his oneness and wholeness to a shattered and broken world.

GENDER ROLES ARE not made up of a list of absolute do's and don'ts. Some well-meaning believers have developed a legalistic attitude and approach to the different functions of men and women, and that is far from what I embrace. God gently leads both men and women to devote most of our time in the arenas in which our masculine or feminine gifts and abilities are most fruitful. It is to magnify our contributions as women that he leads us in certain directions, not to minimize or marginalize us.

It's easy to see how this is misunderstood by extremists on both sides of the gender issue. Egalitarians like to point to Galatians 3:28 to substantiate their belief that there is no difference in the roles men and women are to play. That verse reads, "There is neither Jew nor Greek, slave nor free, male nor female, for you are all one in Christ Jesus." This is a clear statement that we are all equally valued and equally saved once we are believers in Jesus Christ—and a marvelous truth that is! But this message does not override all the verses in the Bible that direct men and women into separate arenas of responsibility. It's within those arenas that we find the roles we are to play as the equally valued and forgiven believers we are.

On the opposite extreme, some ultraconservative interpreters of the Word look only at the woman's roles as wife and mother and give birth to the oppression of women and the view that we should remain perpetually "barefoot and pregnant." Although there are blessings in being both, this image doesn't represent woman in all her created glory.

So what is the complete picture? Some of the most exhaustive research on the Christian roles of men and women of which I am aware has been done by Bill and Barbara Mouser, founders of the International Council of Gender Studies (ICGS). Their research is presented in the Bible studies they developed on the *Five Aspects of Woman* and the *Five Aspects of Man*. These and other similar courses help explain the biblical support for these roles. But here's how I simply explained the five aspects of woman to the women of my family:

As we saw when we read the creation story, a woman shares in the mandate to rule the world and subdue it. As mistresses of our domain we have the approval, authority, and power of God to do works uniquely created for us by him. God supports the decisions we make about our homes, jobs, and relationships when we make them according to his will.

Helper-completer is the role given to women by God at the time of creation as revealed in Genesis 2:18. In this role, we are uniquely equipped to contribute to the success or failure of our marriages. We are independent women of God, yes, but when married we're also interdependent with our husbands within the marriage commitment. Only with our support and encouragement can our husbands be the spiritual leaders and providers God asks them to be. They long for our respect just as desperately as we long for their love. And a successful marriage needs both. The unmarried woman also finds many ways to express her helper-completer nature in work and ministry.

Certainly you can see how we are life-givers! This aspect, or role, speaks to the privilege we have as women to bring new life into the world, but it goes far beyond giving birth and nurturing babies to all the things we do to add comfort, joy, and beauty to life. For example, because of courageous pioneer women, schools and libraries were established during the settlement of the Western United States. We are the founders of culture in every existing society. More importantly, as we draw life from God we bring his life into our relationships; we are life-givers as we share his life with others.

As ladies of wisdom, we can stand up for what's right in this world and draw lines our husbands and children will never cross when we draw them with conviction. A woman who fears the Lord is a vehicle for a particular body of wisdom that God sends to the world through her. In Proverbs 9 we read about the lady of wisdom as compared to the lady of folly, and see how important it is for wise women to take a stand for God's truth. This wisdom archetype is completed in Proverbs 31:31 with praise for the woman who fears the Lord and clings to his truth. "Give her the reward she has earned," we read, "and let her works bring her praise at the city gate."

In 1 Corinthians 11:7 we read that "[man] is the image and glory of God; but the woman is the glory of man." The glory of man aspect was the hardest role for me to comprehend and embrace, because we all want to bring glory to God! However, I came to understand that men are to bring glory to God by reflecting his attributes of compassion, strength, justice, etc. Women are to bring glory to God by reflecting the attributes of the believer as seen in Jesus Christ: surrender, responsiveness, strength found in power under control, purity, etc. We are the glory of man in the sense that when we fulfill our God-given purposes, men are free to fulfill theirs, and all bring glory to God. The beauty and power of our sexuality is all a part of our glory-of-man aspect—and a mysterious and wonderful part it is.

The five aspects of men correlate to those of women as part of God's perfect design. Men are called to be lords of the earth, husbandmen, sages, and the glory of God. Their roles support and sustain women in our roles in every way as they strive to do meaningful and productive work, provide spiritual leadership and financial stability for their families, and protect and nurture their wives and children. They also strive to fight for what's right, to be keepers and purveyors of wisdom, and to love their wives as Christ loves the church.

You may think you've slipped back through time to the days when knights fought for fair maidens and leading men in Hollywood swept young starlets off their feet and gave them just one chaste kiss. But it's not that simple. For one thing, these roles are ideals. None of us can fulfill all these roles perfectly because we live in a fallen world and a fallen culture. The fallen mistress of the domain may face a messy house or an impossible schedule at work. The fallen helper-completer might insist on doing everything herself and render her husband useless and impotent. The fallen life-giver may put her own needs ahead of her child's and might even resort to abortion if an unwanted pregnancy ruins her plans. The fallen lady of wisdom may follow the ways of the world, not God's ways, and the woman representing the fallen glory of man might flaunt and misuse her sexuality rather than honor God with it.

Even though you can't achieve perfection, I challenge you to explore these roles and determine whether you may be ignoring one or another. Your greatest fulfillment as a woman will come when all five roles are evident in your life (though some may take precedence over others in certain seasons). They all reside within your heart of hearts—and the one that may seem most foreign to you may be the one God is asking you to discover. Don't be afraid.

If something in the above paragraphs pierced your heart because you realized you have devoted a good part of your life to fighting gender differences instead of embracing them, you are not alone. I was angry at God when my eyes were opened for the first time—angry that he had allowed me to live so much of my life making mistakes in the dark. But my anger finally gave way to gratitude—gratitude that I now truly understand what happened to create those wounds labeled divorce and single parenthood; gratitude that I can

NANCY

share the truth I now know with my daughters-in-law, stepdaughters, and granddaughters with the fervent prayer that they might embrace and enjoy their feminine roles.

One of the most beautiful metaphors for the blending of masculine and feminine roles is seen in the graceful skill of the ice-dancing couple. Perfectly in sync with one another, he leads and she follows. Mutual trust and communication are essential. He is strong enough to lift her up and exalt her, but she must stay balanced and land on her own two feet gracefully. She leans on him when necessary, but he stays acutely sensitive to her every movement. In complete harmony they glide through their dance, creating something far grander and far more glorious than either of them could create alone.

RECONCILING OUR DIFFERENCES

Regardless of the differences we expressed about what it means to be a woman, we both enjoy being women. And although we have come to different conclusions regarding a woman's ultimate identity, we are both convinced of her value and importance to God—she is utterly loved by him.

Chapter 2

Saying I Do

The Design of a Wife

Love creates an "us" without destroying a "me."
—LEO BUSCAGLIA

WHO OR WHAT IS A WIFE?

NANCY

ALL FOUR OF our children were married within a period of five years. In each instance I was privileged to see the bride just before she took that long walk down the aisle. Forever in my memory are the tears in the eyes of my daughter-in-law Maria as she gazed into her father's eyes in the foyer of the church. My daughter-in-law Abigail was radiating with joy when I peeked in on her and her bridesmaids in the last stages of preparation. She looked like a little girl on Christmas morning! My stepdaughters Joelle and Julie both alternated giggles and tears before their wedding marches.

Isn't it the same with the brides you know? The wonder, the mystery, the joy, the romance, and the hope resonate together in the feminine heart of the woman preparing for her special day.

In a secular sense a wife is anyone who commits herself in marriage to a man, whether at the end of a long church aisle or in the county courthouse. But we can see in the eyes of each bride that she is so much more. Whether she knows it or not, in God's perfect plan a wife is a true woman who embraces her femininity and determines to submit herself to her husband in order to know the fullness of God's sovereignty and love, the completeness of the union of husband and wife, and the very freedom of her own spirit.

My own understanding of what it is to be a godly wife began with experiencing what it isn't. Following my first trip down the aisle, I understood little of the concept of submission. My second marriage has had Christ at its center from the very beginning. Eight years into it God revealed his plan for wifely submission to me and sealed it in my heart by the Holy Spirit. I saw what being a submissive wife was and why submission was so critical to God's plan for a successful Christian marriage—and that truth has made all the difference.

Since the moment Eve decided to listen to the serpent, women have fallen victim to carefully crafted lies. No wonder so many of us watched our marriages dissolve in shambles around us after believing the lies of the feminist movement. Lies like "you can have it all" and "marriage is oppressive." As K. T. Oslin sang in her song "80's Ladies": "We've said 'I do' and we've signed 'I don't' and we've sworn we'd never do that again."[1] I can only wonder how many women are still in the darkness, still looking back at failed marriages with bitterness and confusion, still wondering what went wrong and what would have made it right.

I believe that a Christian wife is one who understands that when she said "I do" to her husband, she was also saying "I will" to the Lord. She was saying, "I will look to your Word for guidance. I will trust in your sovereignty in the good times and when things go wrong. I will create an atmosphere in our home that allows me to express my femininity and supports and respects my husband's masculinity. I will be to my husband his helper, his completer, and his safe, soft place to fall. I will create a home for my husband and children that is a sanctuary of comfort, not a camp of contention."

Clearly men and women are uniquely and differently created. A Christian wife embraces those differences, knowing that she must fulfill her role well and support her husband in his. She rests on the solemn promise of God that they are coheirs in Christ. Her focus is not on how to outwit or dominate her husband, but on how to have what is described in I Peter 3:4 as a "gentle and quiet" spirit around him, for this is of "great worth in God's sight." Not intended to portray a shrinking violet,

NANCY

this is a description of a woman who has respect for authority and a heart for resting in God's will.

Peter goes on to say, "For this is the way the holy women of the past who put their hope in God used to make themselves beautiful. They were submissive to their own husbands, like Sarah, who obeyed Abraham and called him her master. You are her daughters if you do what is right and do not give way to fear" (1 Peter 3:5–6).

Knowing that there are many who disagree with what I believe to be the role of the Christian wife, it would have been easy for me to "give way to fear" and write something far less controversial than this book. But the Holy Spirit wouldn't let me. He wants me to share the truth I've learned about the freedom and rewards of following God's plan for women and to assure every woman that, regardless what others may say or think, God's truth will make her beautiful—as a bride and as a wife.

ALICE

THE WOMAN ACROSS the road washed her windows every day in summer and as often as the cold, dank days of a German winter would allow. I watched incredulously as one who got around to this chore when I could no longer avoid it—when the rays of the sun were at such an angle that they illuminated the dusty, grime-laden panes. Even when I lived in that country, nothing could woo me into window washing. I have kept for posterity, and with some amusement, the commemorative Haus Frau stamp that the government issued in honor of the housewife.

I am adamant that the definition of a wife is not that of a housewife. Over the years, I have worked diligently to disabuse myself of this designation. Whether it is on an official form that requests the entry of the wife's occupation or a reference in a bio, I firmly hold out that I am not married to my house—homemaker may be acceptable—but not housewife.

With over half of all marriages ending in divorce and the very definition of marriage under threat of enormous changes due to ever-increasing pressures to approve same-sex unions, it has perhaps never been more important than it is now to understand what a wife really is.

It's certainly not what it used to be. In an article titled "Conditional Surrender," Rebecca Mead recounts, "A hundred and sixty years ago in Arkansas, a man found himself in need of a wife and placed a plainspoken but eloquent advertisement in his local newspaper: 'Any gal what got a bed, calico dress, coffeepot and skillet, knows how to make britches, can make a hunting shirt, and knows how to take care of my children, can have my services till death parts both of us.'"[2]

The wife of the twenty-first century has a much murkier mandate so maybe that explains, in part, the appeal of certain resurrected teachings regarding women's roles. These current teachings do not dictate nor define the correct role of a wife any more than the teachings that I knew in my day as a young wife. One writer even advocated that wives wrap themselves in Saran Wrap to greet their spouses when they return from work. A friend of mine relates trying this tempting technique on her husband, a gynecologist. He walked right past her saying that he saw naked women's bodies all day, every day, and he would prefer his wife dressed when he came home.

The family matriarch in the movie *My Big Fat Greek Wedding* epitomizes a wife in charge by manipulating her husband while letting him think he is the head. A manipulative, scheming, seemingly in-charge spouse is not an accurate descriptor of a wife either.

Perhaps a wife is defined by her faithfulness. I have the increasingly rare distinction of being married to the same man for over forty-five years. But, unless a long-standing relationship is evolving, healthy, and fulfilling, then longevity in marriage still does not define a wife.

References such as "the better half," "the boss," or "the little woman" all serve to slot the wife into the kind of a role that erodes any chance of establishing mutuality in the marriage relationship. And mutuality is what we are after. So if the honor of being designated housewife, having an enduring monogamy, settling for the role of subordinate spouse, or taking charge fall short of defining who or what a wife is, then what does define her?

She is a person with individual gifts and talents, traits and tendencies that should never, must never, be sublimated to another. The One on whom no one could look and live in the biblical past, now lives in every flawed and frail human believer in equal measure. A woman does not receive a lesser or secondary Savior. When she becomes a wife, she does not lose that standing. Christ has chosen to live in her so that he might come out clothed in her own particular personality, not as a poor second to, or a shadow of, her spouse.

The entire mantra of family values must come under the microscope of heaven. A thought-provoking article by Gretchen Gaebelein Hull, "Jesus and Family Values," presents a rather radical view on Jesus and the family that helps the wife of today bring some perspective to the traditional hierarchical models and to the changing mores of the twenty-first century. "Jesus seemed strangely insensitive to blood relationships (Mark 3:31–35) and to family rituals (Luke 9:59–62). Jesus also called men and women to leave their families and to follow him for extended periods of time."[3] Jesus spoke of the kingdom more than he ever did family. In fact, families were people whom you forsook in order to follow him.

Today's wife will have to face head on some sacred cows if she is to follow her heart as well as her natural Creator-endowed proclivities. Is a wife the only one who can cook, for example? Maybe she hates cooking and her husband does it better. My colorful friend Christa tells of this truth tapping at the window of her heart over the years and the light finally breaking through during the football season. "I loved football as much as my husband did, yet I repeatedly missed out on the game while waiting on him hand and foot—fixing snacks, popping beer caps, and making supper. Wait a minute. Something is not right here! I closed the kitchen and plunked myself on the couch beside him. No supper served in our house that night. Dinner was in a restaurant despite the protestations."

Maybe the wife is much more fiscally responsible and she should keep the books. Many husbands are reckless spenders and money burns a hole in their pockets. "He never thinks about paying off a bill when he gets a bonus, but instead buys a new gadget!" bemoans a close friend. Perhaps the wife is much more adept at conflict resolution than her "appointed head." Does she sublimate her gifts and talents just because she may be straying into her husband's territory? A wife should not stand by and let her husband behave in a toxic and damaging manner simply because of his gender. Think of Abigail who defied her churlish husband's behavior and plunged in to execute damage control (1 Sam. 25:32–38).

A Christian wife is a new creation in Christ—he is in her and she is in him. God's assessment of her is not according to gender. Neither is a man considered as male—he is as much the bride of Christ as is the woman. Life in Christ is not a gender-divided deal.

Must a Wife Submit to Her Husband?

NANCY

AS A YOUNG girl of the '50s I enjoyed sitting in the den with my dad watching TV before dinner. A budding journalist, I wanted to watch the evening news while my sisters quickly left the room after *Leave It to Beaver*. I especially enjoyed hearing my dad's opinions about political events in distant places. But part of the experience was not so positive.

Whether he was enjoying the "sweet tea" of the South or the first of the two bourbon and waters he allowed himself in the evening, he would rattle the ice if his glass was empty. My mother, in the kitchen working to put dinner on the table, would drop whatever she was doing and come get my dad's glass to give him the refill he wanted. Soon she was back, the second drink in hand.

"I will never let any man treat me like such a servant," my nine-year-old soul registered. To this day, if I hear ice rattling in a glass it sends chills up my spine. But because I was offended by my dad's rudeness on this or other occasions, and mistakenly thought it indicative of a marriage based on submission and headship, I failed to see the beauty of their relationship beyond its shortcomings. I missed the larger view of submission and headship they modeled through over forty-five years of marriage—a marriage that nurtured them both and could have positively shaped my whole life had I been paying attention.

Is a wife supposed to submit? Only if she wants to bring glory to God through her marriage. Only if she wants to know complete freedom from the need to be in control and the fear that surrender invokes. If that's what she wants, then she will have to choose to submit herself to God's will, which means submitting to her husband in marriage.

The secular definition of submission is: "To lower. To yield to governance or authority." Christian submission is about yielding your will to God's. It's not about lowering yourself to anyone other than him. Rather it's about making choices that support his design for a man and a woman.

"There is only one thing God wants of us, and that is our unconditional surrender," Oswald Chambers wrote.[4] Our ability to fully embrace our redemption, with all its accompanying rewards, is directly related to our ability to fully surrender—even in the areas where it may seem least convenient, and least natural. We sing, "All to Jesus I surrender, All to Him I freely give," yet in our humanness we are often tempted to withhold a part of self for self alone.[5] For the egalitarian woman, the part withheld is frequently submission to her husband.

I understand how this happens. The misguided woman confuses the fact that men and women are equally valued in the eyes of God and equally saved by the blood of Christ with the fact that they have been given different responsibilities in God's divine plan. But a difference in function does not equate to a difference in worth, nor to any sort of subservience of women.

With my early misunderstanding of submission, fueled by the equality fires of the feminist movement, it's no wonder I initially recoiled from the very word submission, much as my egalitarian sisters do today. Author P. B. "Bunny" Wilson describes her own reaction to this misunderstood word in her book *Liberated Through Submission*. Bunny is married to songwriter and record producer Frank E. Wilson of Motown fame. Early in her marriage, she appeared to be a submissive wife outwardly, but inwardly she struggled. When she turned in her Bible to Ephesians 5:22, where God directed Paul to write, "Wives, submit to your husbands as to the Lord," Bunny's honest reaction was, "Why would God mess up a good book with a Scripture like that?"[6] But she came to learn, as have I, that God used the S word intentionally, and that it is the word that holds the key to understanding and fulfilling not just God's design for a marriage between a man and a woman, but his plan for redemption.

All believers know surrender is the key to living the Christian life. In Ephesians 5:21 we are asked to "submit to one another out of reverence for Christ," so submission is not a foreign concept to the Christian walk at all. Only when it involves wives submitting to their husbands do the hackles seem to go up—but unnecessarily so. When we submit to what God asks of us, we're submitting to his authority first.

In Ephesians 5:1 Paul instructs the believers in Ephesus to "be imitators of God." His detailed instructions of how this should look to the world follow, including his instruction for wives to submit to their husbands. When we realize what a privilege it is to serve God by imitating him, and so submit willingly, we are modeling for the world the kind of obedience and submission Christ displayed when he went to the cross—we are being imitators of him.

How can a woman read Ephesians 5:22 and not believe that God is asking her to submit to her husband just as he asks her to submit to his own authority? Even when she goes to the original Greek text the instruction is the same. There she will find the word *hypotassō* used for submit. If she studies further, she will see that every passage that deals with the relationship of the wife to her husband in the New Testament uses this same Greek verb. And every time this verb is used in the Bible it is used to describe the relationship of submission to an authority.

We see a form of it used in I Peter 3:1-2 where Peter writes, "Wives, in the same way be submissive to your husbands so that, if any of them do not believe the word, they may be won over without words by the behavior of their wives, when they see the purity and reverence of your lives." This is one of many divine reasons for wifely submission, and it involves submission to the authority of a husband who is not even a believer.

In Colossians 3:18 we read, "Wives, submit to your husbands, as is fitting in the Lord." In Titus 2:5 older women are instructed to train the younger women in the church "to be subject to their husbands, so that no one will malign the word of God."

We can't get around it. God said what he meant to say. Men have been given the authority in the marriage, the family, and the church, and women are to allow them to lead in these areas. If we don't, his plan can't be fulfilled—and yet even within the church are those working to foil his design.

I believe that, as daughters of Eve, women are not only capable of being mistresses of deception, we are also capable of being mistresses of exception. "I'm giving up sugar," we tell ourselves, "except for birthday cake, of course. I have to have a piece of my son's birthday cake, don't I?" The Christian wife may think she is submitting to her husband's godly leadership but find that in reality she's submitting "except when I'm sure I'm right and he's wrong" or "except if it's in an area where I clearly have more knowledge."

Obviously, marriage involves sacrifice and dedication on the part of both the husband and the wife if it is to succeed, and God knew that. That's why he also instructed husbands to "love your wives, just as Christ loved the church and gave himself up for her" (Eph. 5:25). Clearly it is easier to be submissive wives if we are married to men who dedicate their lives to loving us as Christ loved the church. An insightful husband will make sure the marriage is a partnership and may even ask his wife to perform tasks for which she is better suited than he. But men are no more perfect than we are. Like us, they may see the path the Lord has laid out for them to follow, but they, too, will occasionally be diverted by their own selfish needs or the false messages of the world.

That's why it's impossible to be a submissive wife without a firm belief in and reliance on the sovereignty of God. Women cannot change their husbands any more than the men can change their wives. The only one who can change any husband is the God who created him. But we can change our response to those husbands.

Bunny Wilson frequently speaks to women's groups about her personal struggle to stay in control instead of submitting to God's will for her marriage. She particularly struggled with wanting to reinvent her husband—his use of time, his decisions, his child-rearing style, etc. But try as she might, no significant change occurred in Frank. Finally she decided to get out of the way and let God have a clear shot at him, and the changes she prayed for followed.

In her best-selling book *The Power of a Praying Wife*, Stormie Omartian addresses this same issue. "Our goal must not be to get our husbands to do what we want, but rather to release them to God so he can get them to do what He wants."[7]

While I was working on this chapter Jim and I escaped on a weekend anniversary trip to the mountains. Over dinner I asked him if there were specific instances he could remember when I had been submissive.

"I remember when you agreed to change churches right after we were married," he said. "I know it was hard on you to leave your church and it meant a lot to me that you trusted my spiritual leadership in that decision. Otherwise, I just remember lots of times when you've said, 'Here are my thoughts, but the decision is yours to make.' That helps me so much, and I'm really grateful for your attitude."

I have to confess, it's not always easy to respond to every situation with an attitude of submission. Obedience to God is seldom easy. My natural inclination, just like that of most women, is to cajole, plan, or manipulate until I get my own way. I came by this naturally! In Genesis 3:16 we find the two-part curse God gave to woman after the fall. After telling her that he would greatly increase her pain in childbearing he says, "Your desire will be for your husband, and he will rule over you." There have been many interpretations of the word desire in this verse, but the one I believe is accurate is that women are cursed with the desire to control their husbands. We see this same idiom used in Genesis 4:7 when Cain is warned that his sin is crouching at the door and "desires to have you." Our curse is that we long to control our husbands, even as we are called to submit to them.

Women struggle under this curse in many ways. Some outwardly succeed in dominating their husbands, as witnessed by the preponderance of TV commercials showing the manipulative, controlling wife and the buffoon husband. Others use more subtle, yet equally unflattering, techniques to make sure they get their own way.

Yet by the grace of God it's possible to behave differently. When I disagree with Jim I make a conscious decision to give him my input in a prayerful, studied way, and then draw on the power of the Holy Spirit to trust God with the outcome, even if it's not what I would have chosen.

So how does this work for me, you and Dr. Phil may ask! Actually, I estimate that Jim makes the decision I would have made 80 percent of the time. Another 15 percent of the time he makes a decision I wouldn't have made, but in the end I see that it was the right one. That leaves approximately 5 percent of his decisions that would give me a chance to say, "See, I knew you should have taken my advice!" But if I discipline myself not to say that, somehow the Lord redeems even those situations in time. You see, it's not about how it works for me, it's about how it works for God. I just have to stay out of his way.

When women choose to submit they aren't putting all their faith in a sinful, human man, no matter how wonderful he is as a husband. They are putting their faith in the power and sovereignty of God. Through their willing, selfless submission they are glorifying God by saying, "Because I trust that what you say is true, and that what you asked me to do is in my best interest, I will submit to my husband."

I take heart in believing that God wouldn't set up a plan like this without also holding men accountable. I know I am privileged to be married to a man with the track record I cited above. But even women who are married to less godly men than my Jim can submit to their husbands without fear (unless they are being abused—which is never acceptable), knowing that whatever shortcomings they see in their husbands they can take to God in prayer—and then watch him do his marvelous work.

We know that it is in our times of weakness as believers that God is strongest. Likewise, we aren't giving up our own thoughts and desires as wives when we submit to our husbands, we are giving them over to God. Our dependence on the sovereignty of God increases when our submissive role is put to the greatest test—and so he is glorified no matter what happens.

Susan Hunt has written as eloquently and solidly about the role of the submissive Christian wife as any writer I've been privileged to read. In her book *By Design* she writes: "Submission, whether it is to God, to one another, to husbands or to male leadership in the Church, is a grace-empowered virtue of humility and reverence for God. It has nothing to do with superior/inferior status or equality. It has to do with attitude and function."[8]

My heart aches for my sisters in Christ who are so afraid to give submission in marriage a try. How discouraging it must be to live under the burden of the need to maintain control and the fear of not being "equal." How sad that they are missing the opportunity to have an incredible partnership with the Lord by helping him mold their husbands to be the men they were designed to be in his way, not as the world would mold them. How tragic that by withholding their husbands' God-ordained right to be leaders in their marriages they are robbing them of the confidence and God-esteem that is rightly theirs. Saddest of all, by holding on so tightly to what they refuse to relinquish, these women are missing the liberating freedom that comes from truly surrendering all to the God who loves them and wants only his best for them.

"What glorious liberty exists when we apply the principle of submission to our lives!" Bunny Wilson writes. "Defenses come tumbling down. We stand totally open before the Lord and others. We abide in constant fellowship with His Spirit. Through submission, we can know what it means to be truly liberated. We can be filled with faith, free at last to become everything God created us to be!"[9]

Submission is a liberating choice, not a shackle of subordination. Any last reservations I had about my call to submit to my husband vanished when I truly embraced the message of Philippians 2:5–8: "Your attitude should be the same as that of Christ Jesus: Who, being in very nature God, did not consider equality with God something to be grasped, but made himself nothing, taking the very nature of a servant, being made in human likeness. And being found in appearance as a man, he humbled himself and became obedient to death—even death on a cross!"

If Jesus could be submissive on my behalf, surely I can submit to my husband in order to reflect the glory of my Lord.

THE PLACE TO look for the answer to the controversial question of submission is certainly God's Word. The trouble is that we have started in the wrong part of the Bible to establish most of our theses on the roles of men and women, wives and husbands. Although the book of Genesis comes at the front of the Book, it is not the beginning of the account. The relationship of Adam and Eve and the subsequent fall to which both sides of the aisle appeal to substantiate their claims, is preceded and superseded by a far greater event that radically changed the course of human history.

The account of God's intention for his creation is recorded in the book of Ephesians—no, not the contested contents of chapter 5 with its references to the marriage relationship, but in chapter 1. We were known, chosen, and planned for from before the foundation of the world, just as Jesus was the Lamb slain from the foundation of the earth (Rev. 13:8). Hear the glorious words of Paul as recorded in this first chapter of the letter to the church at Ephesus: "Long before he laid down earth's foundations, he had us in mind, had settled on us as the focus of his love, to be made whole and holy by his love. Long, long ago he decided to adopt us into his family through Jesus Christ.... He set it all out before us in Christ, a long-range plan in which everything would be brought together and summed up in him, everything in deepest heaven, everything on planet earth" (Eph. 1:4–10 MSG).

As I put those words on the page, they dance before my eyes. My heart soars with joy. Jesus

Christ's death on the cross was already an accomplished fact in the mind of an eternal Father. It was that cataclysmic event, and the resurrection that followed, that would demolish every man-made designation of our fellow humans, lay low every dividing wall of caste and creed, and create a level playing field. What a concept! Distinction no longer exists between Jew and Greek, slave and free, male and female—all of whom were enormously divided at the time of Paul's writing (Gal. 3:28).

The meaning and import of this awesome edict then lies in how we appear to, and are designated by, God. Yet the complementarian response to this thundering pronouncement of Galatians 3:28—often referred to as the Magna Carta of Christianity, the culmination of our redemption—is to insist that the scriptural references to submission and headship take precedence.

The Bible teaches that even from the beginning of humankind's history, both sexes share full and equal partnership. For example, the term "helper" used to describe the position of woman to man (Gen. 2:18) comes from the Hebrew word *ezer*, and is the same word used of God in relation to his creation, so certainly there is no implication of inferiority even back then. Basing a theology of man and woman and their relationship on the descriptive outcomes of sin and treating the consequences as prescriptive is flawed to the point of heresy.[†]

[†] Only the ground and the serpent were cursed, by the way. God's original intent was not to build human relationships on the failure of humankind or even on the original innocence of Adam and Eve, but to build on the cornerstone of his son Christ Jesus who was the first of the new creation race.

I vividly remember when I dared to demur with the leader of one of the women's seminars I attended many years ago. As she espoused the flawed philosophy that relegated women to secondary status, I protested, "Surely the submission and headship thing was only instituted because of the fall?" In the silence that followed the launching of that proverbial lead balloon, I realized that I had inadvertently challenged an impenetrable buttress. I cried all the way home.

Both husbands and wives are participants in submission and their voices should be equally heard in the home. When one voice attempts to override another, then egos clash, hearts harden, and unbent wills tangle the woof and warp of the very fabric they are trying to weave. Married life is a veritable minefield of explosives from which we will never be free in this lifetime. It is a crucible for learning to live by the power of the indwelling life of Christ. When a wife knows who she is in Christ, then she can stand behind healthy boundaries that allow her to live in mutual submission with her husband without relinquishing one iota of her identity. She will do it because the Life in her motivates the highest kind of love that does not seek its own way and never fails. In addition, it never enables another's pathology.

Now if she wants equality and mutuality in marriage, then a wife must take full responsibility for her own life, actions, and the outcomes. No sheltering under the hole-riddled umbrella of "My husband told me." No disingenuous submission as a Southern belle acquaintance of mine gloated triumphantly, "Girl, do you know how much power there is in submission?" That this is a mighty mode of manipulation seemed to have totally escaped her notice.

From his book *Families Where Grace Is in Place*, Jeff VanVonderen very lucidly lends light to the historical context at the time the letter to the Ephesian church was written—the letter from which requirements for submission are extracted. "Wives were already placed under their husbands as a function of their culture. Wives were there to keep the house and take care of the kids. Ephesian husbands went to other women for sex, companionship, even heightened religious experiences. This ... went across the grain of everything an Ephesian man ever learned, every man-woman relationship he ever saw."[10]

The model of marriage that Paul writes of in his Epistles is not so much a model for us to live by, but a showcase to display God's unconditional love—a love to which God is forever committed from eternity past. The picture of the marriage union speaks about God and us—the entire church—as Paul writes, "For we are members of his body. 'For this reason, a man will leave his father and mother and be united to his wife, and the two will become one flesh.' This is a profound mystery—but I am talking about Christ and the church" (Eph. 5:30–32).

By applying this Scripture primarily to the marriage relationship—instead of to the mystery of the union of Christ and the church—religion has perpetuated the division of the body whereas

God's intent was to bring us together. The result of the wrong emphasis is that we all recoil in rejection, curled up in our respective corners of the church.

— ALICE

Should a Wife Support Headship?

IT IS IMPOSSIBLE to discuss submission without discussing headship because the two are designed to work together. Just as women are called to submit to their husbands in marriage, men are called to assume positions of leadership, or headship. One of the key Scriptures establishing God's plan for headship is Ephesians 5:23–24 where we read, "For the husband is the head of the wife as Christ is the head of the church, his body, of which he is the Savior. Now as the church submits to Christ, so also wives should submit to their husbands in everything."

How disheartening it is that our culture has obscured the profound and eternal meaning in these verses. Don't you see? Men and women have the privilege of picturing for the world the relationship of Christ with his church. When a woman submits to her husband's headship, she is showing the world the responsive, submissive heart the believer is to have for Christ.

Many are puzzled by the verses in Mark 12:25 where Jesus explains that "when the dead rise, they will neither marry nor be given in marriage; they will be like the angels in heaven"—but when

— NANCY

we remember that our earthly marriages were created to reflect the relationship of Christ with his church, the meaning becomes clear. This holy marriage is beautifully revealed in Revelation 19:7: "For the wedding of the Lamb has come, and his bride has made herself ready," and again in Revelation 21:9: "Come, I will show you the bride, the wife of the Lamb." The union of Christ with his church is complete in Revelation 22:17, where it is proclaimed, "The Spirit and the bride say, 'Come!'" Once we are united with Jesus, the metaphor of the earthly marriage will be obsolete—so marriage as we know it isn't necessary in heaven. How sad for women to miss the best opportunity we have to reflect the holiness of heaven on earth—the opportunity to be a submissive wife to reflect the believer submitting as the bride of Christ.

Often the behavior God expects of us is modeled for us in the heavenly realm. So it is with submission and headship. As we see above, the New Testament compares the husband's headship over the wife to Christ's headship of the church. If we subscribe to the mistaken line of thought that headship was a result of the fall, not part of God's initial design when he created woman from man, for man, and brought her to man, we lose its greater meaning. In fact, those who say that women have come out from under the authority of male headship are essentially saying that the church has come out from under the authority of Christ! To the extent either may be true, the results are disastrous.

Writing in his definitive work *Men and Women, Equal Yet Different*, Alexander Strauch says, "The basis for the husband's headship is not first-century Roman culture; rather it is Christ and His Church. Here is the most compelling argument that headship in Christian marriage is not cultural but is divinely planned: The husband is the head of the wife as Christ is the head of the church."[11]

A great deal of discussion over the meaning of head in all the verses referring to the man being the head of the wife has ensued over the years of debate over gender roles. Evangelical feminists contend that *kephalē* really means "source" or "origin" without the connotation of headship. However, as Strauch points out, the Greek word for head is *kephalē*, which means literally the head of the body but is used in the figurative sense of "one in authority over" or "leader." Strauch points to research by respected scholar Wayne Grudem, which included over 2,300 uses of the word in ancient Greek, all of which applied to people with governing authority.[12]

My confirmation of the importance of both submission and headship is grounded in the example supplied by the Trinity and in my own life experiences and those of women I know.

While marriage is never used in the Bible as a metaphor for the Godhead, we can find within the relationships of God the Father, Son, and Holy Spirit a model for how headship is to work on earth. In the holy authority structure the Holy Spirit submits to the Son and the Son submits to the Father—yet each is equally God. The three work within this authority structure to perform different roles. In the work of salvation, for instance, the Father called us, the Son died for us, and the Holy Spirit indwelled us. With this example so clearly presented throughout the Bible to all believers, why should we find it hard to accept that we, too, are to live and work within an authority structure? What corporation would succeed without someone appointed CEO? What classroom would have order without a teacher in charge? What marriage can thrive when two heads are battling for leadership?

Often I hear of young women frustrated that their husbands don't seem to be showing the initiative and leadership the family needs, especially once children come along. Too often, it doesn't occur to these wives that they are usurping the leadership role in their marriages. If they really want their husbands to lead, they need to create a space in which that leadership can occur.

An extremely bright and gifted young woman named Lisa stood up in my church to talk about her own discovery of the beauty of submission and headship working hand in hand. "I really didn't get any training in how to be a godly wife," she began. "So I went into my marriage with a very willful and independent spirit. As a result, I was not at peace, and my marriage wasn't at peace." After a yearlong Bible study on biblical womanhood, Lisa made a life-changing discovery. "The role God has planned for me in my marriage is so much better than anything I could come up with if I just submit to it—and it's in submission to Christ that I get the power to submit to my husband," she explained. "Because I no longer have to control everything, I'm no longer fearful. I'm free to be the woman I know I'm supposed to be as a wife, as a mom—as me! It's truly beautiful."

In 1 Corinthians 11:3 Paul writes, "Now I want you to realize that the head of every man is Christ, and the head of the woman is man, and the head of Christ is God." Much-debated Scripture verses about a woman's head being covered follow in 1 Corinthians 11:4–7. Most scholars on both sides of the aisle agree that the overall message Paul was sending was that there should be order in the church and anything contributing to chaos was forbidden.

Yet while today's Christian women may not have fancy hat boxes in their closets, Paul's message in 1 Corinthians 11 is one we must never forsake as out of fashion. He's talking about the authority structure that begins in heaven and continues around our own kitchen tables. When women submit to it by choice, they are not relegating themselves to an inferior position, rather they are honoring God by willingly playing out their role in his divine plan.

When you are walking in the protective light of God's love for you as revealed in his design for marriage, you will be permanently liberated and know true freedom—freedom from living in a constant state of tension and contention with your spouse. Freedom from keeping score to make sure you're winning. (Do you really want to be married

NANCY

to a loser?) Freedom from the need to be in control and the fear you won't be.

Blessed is the wife who realizes the value of submission and headship in her marriage, for she is given the privilege of picturing the authority structure of heaven—and the beauty of the bride of Christ—to the world.

ALICE

"I BELIEVE IN male headship unabashedly and unreservedly. The headship of husbands is clearly taught in the New Testament."[13] This sounds terrifyingly regressive from Gilbert Bilezikian, professor emeritus of Biblical Studies at Wheaton College, an able and articulate advocate of the egalitarian position. However, he is quick to go on to say that we do not quote him in this regard without the rest of the story.

He agrees that a basic tenet of sound hermeneutics requires that the biblical text not be given meaning that does not belong to it. His exposition of the thorny thicket that constitutes the hedgerow of headship concludes that the five passages in the Epistles which use the word "head" consistently indicate the opposite of what the English language means by this word.

He writes, "The Fall had made of Adam ruler over the woman (Gen. 3:16). Christ makes of husbands servants to their wives in a 'relationship of mutual submission' (Eph. 5:21). For this reason, I believe in male headship—but strictly in its New Testament definition."[14] When we examine these texts and their contexts, it is clear that Christ is as much the head of the woman as of the man. There is but one mediator between God and humankind: Christ Jesus (1 Tim. 2:5).

In marriage, the maleficent mantle of subjugation smothers the dignity of a wife. Proponents of this view, wives of the enlightened twenty-first century, continue to malign their sisters when they suggest that women are more readily deceived, are mistresses of deception, and require men to interpret truth for them. Reverting to Eve, if she was deceived then Adam was disobedient. Pick one! Thank God she does not have to for she is a new creation in Christ.

Husbands are hurting too, although they may be unaware of it. The untenable, unreal, and unscriptural role of headship is one they were never made to carry, and they will crumble in the way men often do—stonewall or dominate. It vexes me deeply to see a woman wriggle and squirm into obsequious attitudes in order to submit to her husband. When she is so programmed in her subjugated role, she can no longer hear the voice of the Spirit that whispers, "Surrender to me alone."

A subjugation mentality many times results in a wife staying with an abusive spouse. After all, his directives, disdain, or outright physical beatings must be deserved and God-approved. Statistics state that one woman is battered every fifteen seconds in the United States. Many of them are Christians: many of them are wives of pastors. I know of one case where the women in a certain congregation envied the wife of a preacher and cited his consideration, charm, and kindness to her on a regular Sunday morning basis. "I just smile wanly on the outside and ache on the inside at how little they know of this brute to whom I am married, who berates me constantly—Dr. Jekyll and Mr. Hyde."

Speaking of preachers, an engineer girlfriend of mine related this heart-stopping story of a pastor officiating at an Easter sunrise service. As she settled back to bask in the glory of the old, old story of the cross, her bliss was short-lived. He regaled his audience with the tale of—not the risen Christ—but the unsubmissive wife. He said that if she would polish her husband's shoes, for example, she would be amazed at how much better he would treat her.

In a spirit of mutuality, we must be honest and say that wives can abuse husbands too. Abuse is an equal opportunity employer. To say they do so because of thwarted energy or powerlessness is contrived and misleading. Abusive behavior, at the hands of, or by the tongue of, a male or female is intolerable. However, I cannot go so far as to accept the teaching that women by nature constantly attempt to control and dominate their husbands—a notion based on the interpretation of the word *desire* used in the descriptive outcome of life for the woman after the fall. I consulted with a couple of learned Hebrew scholars and they concede that while this word can mean a desire to control, that is but one of several shades of meaning of the word, Hebrew being the highly nuanced language it is. What a woman must remember is that if this is true of her archetype in Genesis, then the corresponding archetype of the man is equally certain—he will always want to dominate.

When a wife manipulates or abuses, it is not because of her desire for her husband, it is for the exact same reason that a husband abuses—selfishness, fear, and an absence of God's love. It is as sad and pitiable to see a browbeaten, fear-struck husband—gored and bleeding by the sharp tongue of a manipulative wife—as it is to see a wife stifled and imprisoned by a controlling and insecure husband.

To take the submission of Jesus to his Father while in human form as eternally binding—as some teach—results in women's relegation for all time as subordinate to the male. Hear these sobering conclusions on this topic from the pen of Kevin Giles in *The Trinity and Subordinationism*. "The recent impetus to understand the Trinity as equal in divinity but subordinate in function or role has arisen exclusively in the context of arguing for the permanent subordination of women, not in the context of a review of history of the doctrine or a reconsideration of biblical texts and their historic interpretation relating to our understanding of the Trinity ... but rather an all-consuming concern to maintain the 'headship' of men. This passion has led to the most dangerous of all errors—the corruption of the primary doctrine of Christianity, the doctrine of God."[15]

The passion of a wife's heart is primarily to be obedient to that doctrine, for it is for freedom that she has been set free (Gal. 5:1). A free wife is strong and sexy. She and her husband are one flesh and have mutual charge of one another's bodies (1 Cor. 7:4). They are tender and nonabrasive, yet living in truth, for they know—deeply and intimately—the one in whom mercy and truth have kissed. Selfishness has no part in their relationship for they desire to please and cherish this beloved person with whom God has united them—they see Christ in their spouse and their honor knows no bounds.

What a difference the right motivation makes. From an internal locus of control, a wife will joyfully choose to be in right relationship to her husband, and whoever can do the task just does it without checking on the gender appropriateness of the action. External demands, rules, and regulations—no matter how euphemistically encoded in a suitable Scripture—will never have the same loving, lasting results as that of a heart in submission to her Savior.

And at last, when this earth-life is over, the day of reckoning will come where, at the bema seat of Christ, every believer will stand to give account of his or her life (2 Cor. 5:10). A wife will stand alone with no husband to vouch for her or to accuse her. She will stand as she has lived—taking full responsibility for her own life.

Reconciling Our Differences

Though we may disagree on the biblical meaning of the concepts of submission and headship, we have both been privileged to experience the joy, the challenges, and the fulfillment that God intends for women to have in their roles as wives. When love is the preeminent ingredient, a woman can thrive in this God-ordained relationship. We highly recommend marriage!

Chapter 3

Giving for a Lifetime
Motherhood

Mother's love grows by giving.
—CHARLES LAMB

TO BE OR NOT TO BE?

"JUST A MINUTE, I'm choicing!" So was coined a brand-new gerund of the verb *to choose* when my three-year-old granddaughter, Alexa, finally responded to her mother's request. Choice, the ability to select freely after consideration, is one of the most powerful endowments entrusted to us from our Creator. It is the operative word when it comes to choosing whether to be a mother. This personal selection determines a woman's motherhood and, with a husband in agreement—in mutuality—the choice becomes both partners' prerogative.[†]

ALICE

For the majority of women motherhood is a joyous choice; other women long to have children but cannot due to a variety of physical limitations or for lack of a spouse. Certainly, God honors the barren woman—often granting her wish to have a child as the Scriptures record in the lives of such notables as Sarah and Hannah. But this is not always the outcome for many would-be mothers. The ache in the heart, the wistful look of longing in the eyes of a childless woman is very real and very painful. There are those who choose to adopt, submit to artificial insemination, or endure fertility treatments in order to quell that longing. The possibilities of conceiving are ever expanding due to modern medical technology.

In an age of increasing numbers of single mothers due to divorce, those who are unmarried also avail themselves of the various options to become a mother. Some years ago a lovely single lass in our church adopted two little Filipino girls, thereby giving them a home and granting her a happy mother heart.

But not every woman wants to be a mother. I remember well the first time I heard a friend voice such a thought. At the time, we were both mothers of several young children. To a besotted mother who adored her children the words of my friend were shocking and bewildering. "I have struggled to love my children, but I can't. I hated

---

† The decision to abort an unwanted pregnancy is not a legitimate choice in escaping motherhood. The initial choice to engage in the process of sexual activity—excepting rape—was the first act of volition. Deciding to rid oneself of the outcome of that decision is not a viable option in the eyes of God.

their arrival into my life." Many women become mothers against their better instincts with resultant regret. I have yet another friend who chose not to have the children she did not want. This was a decision with which she is still at peace even though she is now a widow.

If we are honest, we are curious as to why a woman would not want to be a mother. We find it a little unnatural. But is it? While it is true that little girls seem more at home playing with dolls and boys with noisy trucks, not wanting to have a real live "doll" does not detract from a grown girl's femininity nor throw her womanhood into question. Is she intent on pursuing only a career or travel? Then surely, it is commendable that she realizes a child might not only impede that ambition, but would suffer deprivation due to divided loyalties. Is she scarred and unable to love adequately? If so, the insightful woman who concludes that she is not able to love and nurture to the extent she deems necessary to raise a healthy child is to be commended for her wise decision.

A woman who confronts such issues may be far healthier than her counterpart who unthinkingly—and sometimes regretfully—becomes a mother. Read what the widely recognized author Alice Miller has to say regarding childhood traumas and their lasting effect in her powerful book, *The Drama of the Gifted Child*, "Clinging uncritically to traditional ideas and beliefs often serves to obscure or deny real facts of our life history. Without free access to these facts, the sources of our ability to love remain cut off."[1]

Social scientists also shed some anthropological light on the specificity of maternal instinct. Sarah Blaffer Hrdy observes this as recorded in her mind-stretching book *Mother Nature*: "Now that the generally accepted view that mothers instinctively love their offspring has been toppled, and now that it can be demonstrated (on many fronts) that maternal succor in the human species is anything but automatic or universal, how can we maintain that there is a biological basis to a mother's attachment to her infant?"[2]

As we pry open the apertures of our understanding to include the possibility that nurturing is not the exclusive domain of the female, we cease to consider the woman who chooses not to have children as either warped or odd. With a fresh perspective, we can begin to honor and affirm this woman and, in so doing, release her from the pressures to perform in the maternal arena. The obligation to produce grandchildren grinds down a woman's resolve as well. Would-be grandmothers take note: Are we putting pressure on our daughters if they are reluctant recruits to motherhood?

Just as Jesus said that some men were born eunuchs (Matt. 19:12) and the apostle Paul suggested that to remain single was preferable in order to do the Lord's work (1 Cor. 7:32–35), it can be no less true that women are equally accepted, approved, and loved if they decide not be mothers. For those of our gender who obey the call to take vows of celibacy in order to be married to the Lord, we have the highest admiration.

Mother Teresa's "children" were birthed in the streets of Calcutta. Recall the exchange that Jesus had with the woman who called out from the crowd, "Blessed is the mother who gave you birth and nursed you." His reply, "Blessed rather are those who hear the word of God and obey it" (Luke 11:27–28). When a woman, a child of God, knows that his guidance for her life may include forgoing motherhood, then she is indeed blessed and without reproach in her Father's eyes.

Women are free to make informed decisions in this vitally important area of their lives, and we need to support them in their "choicing."

ALICE

CERTAIN THINGS WERE just assumed on college campuses in the '60s in the South. For instance, it was assumed that if you weren't engaged by the time you graduated from college, you certainly would be soon. Throughout the year special celebrations were held in dorms and sorority rooms as another coed held up her hand to show her ring—and all her friends screamed in excitement, wondering when their turns would come.

I'm embarrassed to say that many of us based our decisions about when to have babies on the basis of what was expected. When my first husband and I were deployed to Germany for our first tour of duty together after we married, our new army friends greeted us with the adage that every young couple stationed there went home with a baby, a Volkswagen, and a grandfather clock. I was

NANCY

pregnant with our first child before we left the States and remember having morning sickness on the plane overseas. The baby was on the way; the Volkswagen and clock soon followed.

I don't recommend making decisions to marry or have children based on the assumption that it's just the right time of life to do either—or because everyone else is doing it. However, I do believe that we can overanalyze both decisions to our detriment and thwart God's purposes at the same time. Take marriage, for instance: Much is being said these days about thirty-somethings in long-term relationships who stop short of getting married. A key reason for this is that they want to make sure the relationship is working before making a commitment. They may even live together before marriage in order to test things out (a strategy that statistics show more often leads to divorce than satisfaction). How sad they don't understand that in part it's the commitment that makes the marriage work.

Likewise, young women and their husbands or significant others spend long hours in discussion deciding on the perfect time to introduce a child to the mix. Will it be after she's established in her career and so can risk taking some maternity leave? How will she measure this "established" status? Will it be after they have saved the money for a down payment on a four-bedroom house in the suburbs? Once one baby comes, will there be a second? If so, when?

All this analyzing and planning has one major flaw: It presumes upon God. God is the Creator of life. All birth control issues aside, it is his call as to who will become a mother and when. He decides whether the baby will be a girl or a boy and whether he or she will be athletically inclined, brilliant, or beautiful. The "designer babies," with gender and physical attributes preselected, may be a coming phenomenon, but even then God will remain in control. He and only he creates life, even if he allows it to take form in a test tube.

Whether to become a mother is one of the most important decisions a woman makes in her life—but it's not one that she can make under the assumption that she will be granted the child she wants when she wants it, and it's not one she can make without God's participation. The truth is that while many of us may have rushed into having children because it was the anticipated "next thing" to do, we never would have had them at all if we had waited for the time when we felt emotionally adequate, financially stable, and well-educated in all the shifting philosophies of parenthood. Do you know who made us adequate, stable, well-educated moms? Our babies did.

Just as God doesn't give us more trials than he gives us the grace to bear, so he doesn't send a child for us to rear without instilling in us an amazing, natural ability to mother that child. But he doesn't send all the knowledge and intuition we need when we're just sitting around the kitchen table deciding whether to have a baby. He sends it just before we pick up our tiny blessing for the first time. He sends it when the baby latches onto the breast that will sustain him and curls his little hand around our fingers. That's when a mother is born, and when she discovers that she is perfectly ready—and no one on earth could be a better mom to her baby than she.

It's heartbreaking when a woman desperately desires to have a baby but, for one reason or another, puts off doing so until it's biologically too late. And only God knows when "too late" will be in each particular case. In order to circumvent this circumstance some young career women are choosing to have their eggs harvested and frozen while they are young, with the intent of taking them out of the fridge and having them fertilized and inserted in vitro later, thus allowing them the option of having babies into their fifties. Even ovaries may someday be removed and frozen for the same purpose. But why? Isn't this the height of arrogant presumption?

Betty Rollin, an author and news correspondent, wrote a very poignant article about the baby she never had and only began to grieve once she turned sixty. Betty began her writing career in the '70s and wrote about the oppression of motherhood in the company of no less than the late Betty Friedan. A few relationships and two bouts with breast cancer later, she began looking longingly at the bond she saw between mothers and babies, but by then it was simply too late.

"I continued to struggle with this nonmotherhood thing," she wrote. "The struggle ended when I stopped struggling. That is, I stopped trying so hard not to be sad. I realized—and accepted—that I'd always be sad about it."[3]

NANCY

Of course there are many reasons women don't or can't become mothers. Infertility can occur at any age. In my view, Christian women also respect that in God's perfect plan, motherhood is preceded by marriage. They don't see motherhood as a decision to be made while looking through the catalog at a sperm bank either alone or with a "life partner" of either sex. God planned for babies to be born of women within the protective boundaries of the heterosexual marriage, period. To orchestrate things differently is to make a decision based on selfish needs for fulfillment, not on what's best for the child. Women without husbands need to consider the blessings of adoption instead.

The decision about whether and when to be a mother is one every woman should make with her husband and God. It's also one she must make as much with her heart as with her head. And trite as it may sound, she should make it knowing there's an element of sacrifice involved in mothering. Not senseless sacrifice, but the kind of unselfish giving that bears fruit long after the mother is gone.

Is Motherhood Necessary for Fulfillment?

ALICE

DURING THE INTENSE real-life drama played out on our TV screens in March 2005, few of us were unmoved by or indifferent to the tragic Terri Schiavo case. A mother had tended to her helpless daughter for fifteen years and was in excruciating anguish as she watched her daughter fade after the removal of the feeding tube. Amongst the thousands of words spoken on Terri's behalf, four stand out as especially significant to me—those of that mother saying, "She is my life."

While we hope that none of us finds herself in such an agonizing scenario, these four words speak volumes to all who look for fulfillment in the noble status of motherhood. Who among us has not expressed such a sentiment at some time? (We have also been known to declare that children "will be the death of me" from time to time as well.)

From the moment of discovering that we are pregnant, to watching in wonder as our bellies swell with new life, to hearing that first cry, and then holding the crinkled soft flesh of our babies—the thrill is indisputable. Just writing these words vividly conjures up for me that blissful experience, even to the way my babies smelled. No wonder we feel that this must indeed be the epitome of fulfillment. Could there possibly be a higher calling? Even celebrity moms say that the arrival of their child capped every other accolade or pinnacle of performance. It is awesome and wonderful. But it is not a prerequisite to fulfillment and is not a substitute for the crowning reason of our lives—it is not the magnum opus of our life.

When we seek to find fulfillment in the role of mother or through our children, we have lost sight of our completeness in Christ. We are not meant to live our life through another, but let another live his life through us (Gal. 2:19–20). Motherhood, despite its joys and undeniable satisfaction, involves wills other than our own; our children will choose differently from us, perhaps even in opposition to our value system. If the formulas we use to raise "perfect" children fail, then our sense of fulfillment will be sorely shattered.

Much of the dogma, devotion, and near deification status around motherhood is not scriptural. I contend that some of this fervor has its genesis in the promise of being the life-giver as pronounced over Eve (Gen. 3:20). This strong undercurrent tugs deeply on the psyche of many earnest religious women. Although the Christian woman truly knows, deep down, that she is only in right relationship to God through Christ, a certain few verses tucked into one of Paul's letters have her thinking that maybe, just maybe, having children will make sure she can atone for being the first to be deceived (1 Tim. 2:13–15). Most biblical scholars agree that "being saved through childbirth" does not mean that a woman's eternal salvation is secured in any other way than a man's is, namely through the atoning work of Christ on the cross and in his resurrection. While a perplexing passage to reconcile with the consistent criterion for becoming a Christian, the prevailing philosophy that Paul is endeavoring to refute was that of the Gnostic position which declared females ineligible to find salvation until they gave up their femaleness. Therefore Richard and Catherine Kroeger, in their eloquent treatise *I Suffer Not a Woman*, suggest that this passage means that, "Women are acceptable to God within their childbearing function and need not change their sexual identity to find salvation."[4]

In the course of writing another book specifically on motherhood, I spoke with many for whom the empty nest period was really the first time they faced the futility of hinging their life's fulfillment on their children. They had to learn that their identity is not in their children's just as their children's is not in them. Others had learned this truth long ago. In the northern islands of my native Scotland, the story was often repeated of how, many years ago, Annie lost her five sons and her husband to the scourge of tuberculosis. To those who heard her singing hymns on her way back up the hill from visiting their graves in the little churchyard by the sea, it was evident that she had her anchor firmly fixed in Christ.

Jesus told the Samaritan woman at the well that he would give living water that would become an everlasting source of supply (John 4:14). That is fulfillment and it has nothing to do with motherhood. The illustrious Greek poet and dramatist Sophocles (495–406 BC) said, "Children are the anchors that hold a mother to life."[5] We know better. We have an anchor that keeps us focused on what constitutes our real life—grounded in heaven. Even if we are never a mother, never reach the ranks of the famous, or never produce a child that becomes president, in Christ Jesus we are entire and undiminished. How good of God to define us according to our essential selves, not our attributes, achievements, or associations.

ONE OF A woman's created purposes is to be a life-giver. For most women this life-giving function is best realized by giving birth to and nurturing children. Our bodies were inarguably created to bear and birth children. Our pelvis is more flexible and wider than a man's so there's room for a baby to grow in the womb. Later, that protruding hipbone is where we balance the little ones we carry. I clearly remember the first time my son nursed at my breast and I realized, quite apart from the male fascination with cleavage, that this was why my body had breasts! Everything about the female body is designed to bear and nurture children.

Yet you don't have to give birth to be a mother. Adoptive moms and stepmothers can be every bit as dedicated to and effective in guiding and loving children as birth mothers. My friend Eileen married a widower with three small children when she was only twenty-three. She raised those children alone after her husband died young and is as devoted a mom as I know. Daily she prays for her two grown children and mourns the stepson who committed suicide in the midst of drug use despite her best efforts to reach out to him. She delights in her grandchildren—when we share advice and ideas, it's as one grandma to another.

However not every woman expresses her life-giving aspect by bearing or rearing a child. Most recently when I think of women who may have made a conscious decision not to marry and have children, U.S. Secretary of State Condoleezza Rice comes to mind. A woman as beautiful and intelligent as she must have had her share of male attention, but she makes it clear that she doesn't believe women can play all roles well at once, and she opted for a political career. Do I think that in the dark of night she sometimes second-guesses her decision? Yes, I do. But do I admire and respect her for making it? Absolutely. Her life-giving role is playing out in the wise decisions she makes as she represents our country to the world and labors to give birth to peace in the Middle East.

Of course she's not the only example of a fulfilled, life-giving woman who has never been a mother in the physical sense. We all know school teachers, nuns, nurses, great aunts, and others who have made life richer for those around them through their gifts of service and nurture. We also give life as we point people to God and nurture them spiritually.

Still, we can't deny that God planted in the heart of the woman the desire to bear children. Were that not so, it would have been impossible for his people to be fruitful and multiply. Over the centuries women have suppressed that desire and rationalized it away in a million different ways. A woman who isn't a mother can find alternate sources of fulfillment, but she also misses a significant part of God's plan for her.

Unless medical complications prevented her, every mother felt when she was wheeled from the delivery room like Queen Elizabeth in her royal carriage on Coronation Day! The euphoria of childbirth is like nothing I've experienced before or since. At that moment, you feel like the only woman ever to give birth and that your child is the

NANCY

most perfect, lovable child ever born. That's the gift God planned for us.

Many very accomplished women have been surprised at how easily they responded to motherhood once they finally gave in to it. Author and columnist Anna Quindlen wrote, "When I quit the *New York Times* to be a full-time mother, the voices of the world said I was nuts ... but if success is not on your own terms, it is not success at all."[6]

Actress Michelle Pfeiffer had given up on love but not on being a mom when, at thirty-four, she adopted her daughter. Soon after, she married her second husband and they had a son together. "The birth of a child changes you," Pfeiffer said. "Suddenly, you're in the presence of a kind of purity. Everything shifts and is honed down to its essence, and you realize that the things you thought were so important are ridiculous. You begin to see what really matters."[7]

Is motherhood necessary for fulfillment? Not absolutely. Is it one of the most satisfying, soul-gratifying choices you can make in order to fulfill your purpose as a woman? Oh, yes.

What Does a "Good Mother" Look Like?

ALICE

ONE OF MY little grandsons gave me the ultimate, unsolicited compliment once as we all sat around the dinner table. "Nanny, you are just like Jesus!" His father (my son) laughed at the pronouncement, perhaps wondering if they were both thinking of the same person! Like most mothers, I did the best I could—and even did it well by most standards—though I confess I was often not very Jesus-like.

The quality of a mother cannot be known by looking at either her or her child. We come in various and sundry shapes and sizes, backgrounds and persuasions. As an insightful pastor once said, "I've seen good children from bad homes and bad children from good homes." The standard by which to measure good is not humankind's or even the church's criteria. What matters is how God measures our good. And good in his eyes is the perfection of Jesus Christ who is now our indwelling life (Gal. 2:20). We cannot improve on that.

Yet even in the realm of motherhood, we continue to push for perfection in our own strength. Questing for the mythical Holy Grail of perfectionism in our own abilities is futile and frustrating. How can we expect perfection when we report for duty still carrying our own personal, psychological, and emotional baggage? Only the heavenly Parent is perfect, and he cares so much more for our children than we do—impossible as that seems—which means that we can trust him to do the job on his own. A good mother lets go and lets God. "Yes," the joke goes, "I have relinquished my position as fourth person of the Trinity, and if you are smart, you won't apply for the job."

Letting go is not easy. In Judy Goldman's novel *Early Leaving*, the protagonist's only son, the adored and gifted Early, for whom she spared no expenditure of time, effort, and love, is now in prison for murder. "I have given up trying to find a formula. If I pray before I go to sleep, wish hard, if I am patient with boring people, if I let the other car cut in, if I donate old coats to Crisis Assistance Ministry, Early will miraculously be released from prison."[8]

The grief that this mother expresses is not hard to identify with. Our concerns may not be quite as dramatic as murder or prison, but whatever disappointment, pain, or prodigal situation we face, we still look for something we could have done better. The hand-wringing words of regret and recrimination are set to the tune of guilt. A good mother changes both the words and the music. She knows that forgiveness flows freely for every mistake, and she clings to the promise of God that assures her of this: "And we know that in all things God works for the good of those who love him, who have been called according to his purpose" (Rom. 8:28).

In response to God's grace, a good mother loves her child with the love of the Holy Spirit (Rom. 5:5). Our natural love, although intense and self-sacrificial, is still limited, flawed, and often toxic. Our brand of loving is often analogous to a hovering helicopter: a fussing, overly solicitous mom trying to manage and oversee every eventuality in her children's lives. Just as the helicopter hovers over its occupants even after they have disembarked, so we often continue trying to control our children even when they are grown and gone, creating the kind of downdraft that causes our offspring to duck out of the way. The current is often so great that they feel helpless to be free of its influence—an influence that haunts them and continues to disturb their adult life.

Hurting our children is the last thing we ever intend to do, of course. However, Christian moms are not immune from the stress that accompanies parenting particularly in this overachieving, highly competitive age in which we live. Stress and angst are rooted in fear. The Bible tells us that love dispels fear (1 John 4:18). The perfect love of the Father for us and for our children eradicates the root of anxiety. In that same letter, the apostle John pronounces that the One who lives in us is greater than all the destructive forces that surround us (1 John 4:4). This is another reason for fear to flee. When we find ourselves fretting over our children's safety or worrying that they are not as involved in activities or sports as our neighbor's child, we are in fear of some form. What a blissful relief to remember the promises of God's Word that pronounce both mother and child as chosen and specially selected members of the body of Christ. Our *real* lives are hid with God in him (Col. 3:1–3). A good mother—that is, one who has come to the end of her own efforts, one whose heavenly Father is teaching her to let go and trust him for her own life and that of her children—has no need to be afraid. This mother will look a little bit like Jesus as he lives his life through her. That makes for the best possible mother in the world.

OBVIOUSLY THERE'S NO definitive description of a "good mother," good being a relative term open to many interpretations. However, we can look at examples of effective, excellent mothering, and we can look at what happens when mothers are not as wise, focused, and balanced as they could be.

As I observe the mothers around me, I believe the best mothers are those who are able to discipline themselves to be present in the moment. They aren't wishing their busy toddlers were teenagers, nor wishing their challenging teenagers were toddlers. They aren't focused on the career opportunities they sacrificed or on how to achieve more acclaim in the world. They are "ordained" mothers in the sense that they know God put them with these children at this point in time and that no one can replace them in their children's lives.

Gigi Schweikert has written several poignant books on motherhood. In one she writes, "Every night I scrub four kids (and sometimes the dog), read just one more story, give four extra kisses, fall into bed, and recognize that the man next to me is my husband (I usually only see him when I whiz by so he looks different when he's not blurry). I close my eyes and ask myself, 'Was I a good mother today?' and a little voice inside me says, 'What do you think?'"[9]

Gigi goes on to say that some days she isn't always sure, and anyone who's been a mom knows those doubts. As a single mom working full time, I was often guilty of squeezing motherhood in between all the other tasks requiring my time and attention. I was also focused on rebuilding my damaged self-esteem after the agony and rejection of divorce, which translated into more evening hours spent satisfying corporate demands and dating than I care to add up.

Years later, after I had remarried and my sons were out of the house, I had an opportunity to go on a long walk with the two of them. I formally asked them to forgive me for not being a "better" mother, listing major failings, like my share of the problems leading to divorce from their father, and minor ones, like serving leftover pizza a few too many times. We hugged, and they forgave. When I asked if there was anything I could do for them then to make their lives better, they suggested a ski boat would be nice. Forgiveness is a beautiful thing—and so is laughter at just the right moment. (And no, they didn't get the boat. I didn't feel that guilty!)

Seeing my sons now as loving, responsible husbands and fathers, I'm so grateful to God for redeeming them, and me, from my shortcomings. And deep in my heart I dare to whisper, "Maybe I did something right."

That "something right" is not so much what we can do, or plan, or orchestrate, as it is offering unconditional love—a love so powerful it can be delivered only in that package of readiness I mentioned above. After my son Rob came through an especially angry, self-destructive adolescence, he asked me why I hadn't given up on him during the tough times. "Because moms can't give up," I said. "It's just not in our job description." I had to employ some tough-love techniques during those years and stop rescuing him so he would suffer the consequences that eventually reversed his behavior. But it was the love for him that God put in my soul that gave me the strength to be tough, too.

My concern for mothers today is that they too often take their cues about what it means to be a "good mother" not from the intuition God gave them, but from the society around them. Moms become competitive about birthday parties, sports, and clothes. Even in certain Christian circles mothers can be competitive instead of being a needed support for one another. One example of this is in the area of homeschooling. I believe homeschooling is a wonderful solution for many families, and statistics tell us well over a million students in the United States are homeschooled. But this option isn't for every family nor every child. It shouldn't be the educational plan of choice if the mother is the primary teacher and isn't gifted in that area. She shouldn't be made to feel guilty if she and her husband decide to send their children to charter or public schools instead.

A "good mom" spends the time necessary to get to know her children well individually. Then she and her husband will make the best choices not only about their education, but about any activities they engage in. It's when a mom tries to do everything perfectly—perhaps adding the necessity or choice of working outside the home to the mix—that she may literally drive herself crazy while driving her kids everywhere else.

In her article "Perfect Madness: Motherhood in the Age of Anxiety," author Judith Warner writes, "Once my daughters began school, I was surrounded, it seemed, by women who had surrendered their better selves—and their sanity—to motherhood. Women who pulled all-nighters hand-painting paper plates for a class party. Who obsessed over the most minute details of playground politics. Who—like myself—appeared to be sleepwalking through life in a state of quiet panic."[10]

If mothers are like this, and I'm convinced many today are, then what of their children? Where's the voice of reason that says two extra activities a week is plenty. Where's the time to have casual conversations in the kitchen or to play tag in the backyard? Hectic days will never cease, but motherhood doesn't have to lead to madness.

A wise mother not only keeps her children from turning into multitasking robots fueled by motherly competition, she also knows how and when to set boundaries for her children. Her discipline is consistent, and she's confident in delivering it. You won't find her asking a two-year-old if he wants to go to bed or waiting for a six-year-old to decide when she thinks it's time to come out of the pool. She's the mom, she's in charge, and her children grow up confident not only in their mother's authority, but in her love—a love that says, "Being your mother is my job, and you can count on me to do it. I don't expect to need any parenting help from you today."

> Moreover, a wise and good mother stays close to God and understands how important it is for children to see biblical womanhood and manhood modeled in the home. She respects her husband the way he needs to be respected and allows him to love her as she needs to be loved. She and her husband make sure the children are consistently in bed at a normal hour, not only for the good of the children, but so they have some time alone together each evening. And she makes time for special dates and romance. For she knows that taking care of her marriage is a large part of taking care of her children.
>
> It's a big job, isn't it? Still, the wise mother realizes that the season of motherhood is one of many seasons in her life, and that motherhood is the most important job she will ever have. Her children will be small only for a short time, and she's their one and only mom. They need her desperately, and she will find within each busy day more than enough blessings to make every sacrifice worthwhile.

Reconciling Our Differences

We are both devoted mothers and grandmothers, and we respect one another's devotion to family, often joining together in prayer for one another's children and grandchildren. While we emphasize different aspects of motherhood based on our opposing views of womanhood, we both hold motherhood in high esteem.

Chapter 4

Finding Our Niche

The Working Woman

I stood up straight and worked my veritable work.
—Elizabeth Barrett Browning

WHEN IS WORK PRODUCTIVE AND SATISFYING?

NANCY

COLLAPSING INTO BED entirely drained is not the same as snuggling under the covers looking forward to some well-earned rest. The difference: satisfaction. A busy day of fruitless activities depletes; a full day of productive and satisfying work satiates. The exhausted woman probably won't sleep well. The appropriately tired woman will.

We were created both to work and to take joy in our work. God gave the mandate to rule the world and subdue it to both Adam and Eve in the garden of Eden—and subduing the world takes work. Yet we feel happiest when we are productive, and achieving a balance of work and rest is the key to successful living. It all depends on the work we choose.

"Honest labour bears a lovely face," bemused poet Thomas Dekker in 1603[1] and we can only surmise he was thinking of women's work. But what is women's work, and how do we make sure that the work we do is both productive and satisfying?

I take great joy in coming across the right person in the right job at the right time. Whether it's a waitperson with a particularly sunny disposition and the gift of service or a dentist who makes the effort to ensure that a filling is in to stay, excellence is a job well done by a person well-suited for that job. At the end of the day, these people know they made a contribution to society. Their job satisfaction shows in the work that they do, because they are equipped to do the job at hand.

In my experience, the most productive and satisfying work we do is the work that is in keeping with our created strengths, natural abilities, and spiritual gifts—and all those job qualifications come from God. Ephesians 2:10 says, "For we are God's workmanship, created in Christ Jesus to do good works, which God prepared in advance for us to do." We aren't saved by works, but we are saved for works—so that we can do our part in God's kingdom on earth. And since he knew in advance the work he had for us to do, we can be sure he's equipped us to do it. Our job is to know ourselves well enough to recognize the assignment God intends for us when he reveals it to us.

The most stressed-out people today, male or female, are those who are working outside of their innate gifts and abilities, outside of their values, and outside of God's plan for their lives. As women who know we were created primarily to be helper-completers and life-givers, we are wise to look for work opportunities that play to those strengths, whether at home or outside the home. Feminists have proven that women can do almost every kind of work men can do—but the real question is whether they should. Is a job in a traditionally male arena the best use of the limited time we have, and is it the work God created in advance for us to do?

Work is most rewarding when we see it as a ministry, whether it's in a secular organization or a Christian home. Colossians 3:23–24 says, "Whatever you do, work at it with all your heart, as working for the Lord.... It is the Lord Christ you are serving." When we develop that mindset and heart attitude, then everything we do—from mopping the floor to balancing a multimillion-dollar corporate budget—has eternal significance and thus a higher standard of excellence.

Rick Warren's book *The Purpose-Driven Life* has sold millions and achieved international acclaim in part because he taps into our innermost desires to make our lives matter. "You were put on earth to make a contribution," he assures readers. "You were created to add to life on earth,

NANCY

not just take from it. God wants you to give something back."2

To the extent we are able to discern what our contribution is to be and to devote ourselves to fulfilling it passionately, we will find that our work is both productive and satisfying. And we will sleep well at the end of the day.

ALICE

WHEN IS WORK productive and satisfying? Some might say when it is finished. And they're in good company. When God completed the cosmos, he said, "It is good." The creating of the flowers, the fauna, and the folks who populated the earth started as a dream in the heart of our Creator. It was orderly and daring. He spoke and it was so. I love this picture of what productive and satisfying work should look and feel like. And, because we—both male and female—are made in his image, we too have dreams to harness into reality. The work assigned to our name is awaiting our action and faith to perform (Eph. 2:10).

We are sometimes reluctant to act because one of the great divides with which we as Christians still struggle is the myth of the secular versus sacred. We have a propensity to categorize certain occupations as the Lord's work—minister, missionary, or evangelist—while we relegate floor manager, engineer, and bank teller to the secular. No such divide exists. God loves and values his entire world, and all the talents that he has given each person are valid and necessary for the orderly running of the earth, which he has given to humans. He did not divide the world up into good or bad places, superior and inferior people, or preferable professions. In Jesus' day, one of the most despised professions was that of tax collector.

For a woman the fields are equally wide, fertile, and ready for plowing. The seed for sowing is already in us, and a harvest of satisfaction is ready to be reaped. It is well past time. The constrictive paradigm that relegates a woman to certain pursuits because of her gender is an outmoded model that belongs to the agrarian-patriarchal past. It is enlightening to read what J. Lee Grady has to say on this from his popular book *Ten Lies the Church Tells Women*: "In the 1800s, before the Industrial Revolution, both men and women worked at home. Most people farmed, fished, or hunted; if they had a trade, their workplace was situated somewhere on their property or in their own house. Men did not get up each morning and go to work after drinking their coffee; their wives did not kiss them at the door and wait for them to return at dinner time."[3] That was the model with which I grew up, so this practice was still in effect well into the post-WWII years and beyond in rural settings.

Now we are familiar with a modern urban setting with all its attendant complexities. Die-hard traditionalists consider letting women out of their broom closets as a construct that abandons

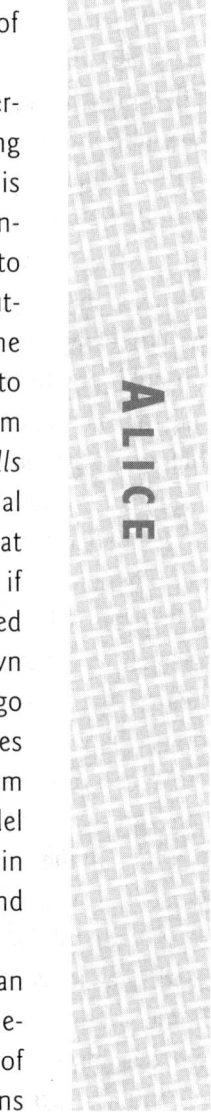

God's original plan, but egalitarians consider the opposite to be true, that trying to return to an untenable division of labor based on an archaic canon—not a divine dictate—is really the true artificial construct.

What is good for all of us is to find work that satisfies. I was raised in a rural setting where the folks held manual activity in higher esteem than sedentary work—a legacy that I have relinquished rather reluctantly. However, I have found after a decade of writing that, for me, the sedentary work of painting a landscape of thoughts and ideas with words is much more conducive to my gifting than pulling early-morning watches for newborn lambs on cold, northern, spring mornings. Our God had already planned the paths of good works for us before we arrived on planet earth. For women that reaches beyond even motherhood—as productive and satisfying as that is.

The passion we have for our work greatly influences what we do. Like the Geiger counter that clicks when it detects radiation, so will our hearts beat faster when we discover what turns us on—when we detect that for which we have been created. Work plays a significant part in shaping our earthly roles. In her book *Women and Men: Gender in the Church,* Carol Penner says, "Our work is also important in developing our identities; it can give meaning to our lives. Some of the work we do is for wages, some not for wages. Some of our work has a clear job description; other work is more difficult to define ... we have the potential to work towards wholeness for ourselves and others."4 As long as we are doing what our Father tells us to do, we are doing something important—no matter what it is.

Part of satisfying work is rest. God modeled this when he rested after creation was complete. Knowing when to take a Sabbath seems to slip our mind and never makes it onto our crowded calendar. The tendency to worship the work ethic has led to a preponderance of people who are workaholics—and the woman working at home is not immune from this affliction. If we are forever cleaning, cooking, or carpooling, the concept of rest is just as elusive to us as to our sisters scrambling up the corporate ladder.

With a schedule too heavy, our children are learning to live life without blank spaces—without wonder time. The limitless opportunities that we enjoy in this nation of enterprise and initiative make the habit of working around the clock seem like a virtue. In some experts' estimation, work compulsion is an addictive behavior. Presenteeism has overtaken absenteeism as a work issue. When we find ourselves in this mode, then we compromise our productivity and our lives become imbalanced. We have then traded our satisfaction quotient for a frustration factor. Busyness can annihilate our hearts.

The product of balance is the thrill of a job well done, the satisfaction of watching the endless variations of creativity that emerge from the great subterranean resources we have in us—Christ, the very Word that created and sustains the universe. Wow! That is exciting. So, off we go to try out a new recipe, write another chapter of a book, or try one more lab experiment to find the cure for cancer. The source is the same, and he fully satisfies us in our work.

SHOULD A WOMAN WORK OUTSIDE THE HOME?

I WORKED OUTSIDE my home from the time my younger son entered kindergarten until he graduated from college. It wasn't until my second husband and I were empty nesters that I felt a longing to go home, accepted a voluntary separation package from my employer, and set up a part-time freelance business out of my home office.

How "backwards" you might say—and in a sense you'd be right. I missed all those afternoons at home after school with my boys when they were growing up. I wasn't able to volunteer for their school field trips or drive them to sports practices. Instead, I checked in by phone and joined the ranks of impatient working women tapping their feet in line at the grocery store at the end of the day hoping no one notices they have too many items for the express lane.

For seven of those sixteen years I was a single mom and needed to have an income, but that's not the only reason I worked. I enjoyed the identity I had at work. I liked putting on "real" clothes every day. I needed the affirmation that my education hadn't gone to waste and my skills were appreciated and useful. I understand all those needs, so I'm not going to launch a campaign for every woman to stay at home every day of her life.

What I am going to suggest, however, is that it's possible to be wiser than I was. It's possible to realize that your life has seasons. In other words, if you have children who are school-age, this may not be the season for you to accept a corporate position that drains you of your energy and robs your family of your loyalty and devotion. Proverbs 14:1 reads, "The wise woman builds her house, but with her own hands the foolish one tears hers down." The decisions we make about whether and when to work outside the home are critical in determining if our households are flourishing or literally falling down around us.

If we do work outside the home, a huge factor in how positive our work experience is for us and our families is whether we are working at a high level of productivity and satisfaction. Carefully choosing the kind of work we do, and with whom, can make the difference between selling our souls for a paycheck and being able to keep an at-home attitude in the midst of an eight-hour workday.

"Women have been liberated right out of the genuine freedom they enjoyed for centuries to oversee the home, rear the children, and pursue personal creativity," wrote Dr. Dorothy Patterson. "They have been brainwashed to believe that the absence of a titled, payroll occupation enslaves a woman to failure, boredom, and imprisonment within the confines of home."[5]

When I look back over my working years I realize that what I enjoyed most about working as a writer was its life-giving creativity. What I enjoyed most about managing a department of writers, editors, and graphic artists was the interaction with people and the opportunity I had to nurture and encourage them. I was in a position that made office politics and corporate maneuvering impossible to avoid, but it was the completing parts of my job that brought me joy, not the competing parts. I was responding to the aspects of my work that put me in touch with my created design as a woman—even though I didn't know it at the time.

The decision about whether to work outside the home is one that a married woman with children can make only in sync with her husband and with God. I often suggest women take a pragmatic approach to the decision by making a list. On one side of a sheet of paper, list all the things you will have to give up if you don't go to work. On the other side, make a list of all the things your children will have to give up if you do. Which list carries more weight?

Many women, even those in esteemed positions with high-paying salaries, are facing this issue and are ultimately deciding that the cost of working outside the home is just too high. A writer for the *New York Times Magazine*, Lisa Belkin, surprised feminists coast-to-coast when she wrote, "There is nothing wrong with money or power. But they come at a high price. And lately, when women talk about success they use words like satisfaction, balance and sanity."[6]

A special report in *Time* titled "The Case for Staying Home" revealed "an up tick in stay-at-home moms who hold graduate or professional degrees—the very women who seemed destined to blast through the glass ceiling." Corporations reported noticing a "brain drain" in the female work force among women earning $55,000 and more. "What we have discovered in looking at this group over the last five years is that many women who have any kind of choice are opting out."[7]

As women, we often have more choices regarding work than we realize. Women are innately creative and resourceful. If spending more time at home is a priority for you and your family, you can probably find a way to make it happen. Ask for part-time hours, work-at-home days, or flextime. Look at the family expenses and find a way to trim them down. Read books like *Miserly Moms* by Jonni McCoy—and become one.

I don't have to look beyond my own family to see how this can work. My daughter-in-law Maria was a mom holding fast to her dream of getting a college degree. She took a few classes consistently once the girls were in school and finally got her degree in education. Now she teaches high school English full time but is able to mesh her schedule perfectly with those of her three daughters. Her income is important to her family, but not nearly as important as her presence in their lives. That she understands that is a blessing to her, to the girls, and to my son Rob.

My daughter-in-law Abigail has been equally creative and resourceful. She gave up a job as assistant art director at a national magazine to go with my son to seminary and become a mom. During the year Tim was studying in Oxford, after they had two children, Abigail picked up a set of watercolors and discovered she had a talent for painting portraits. Just two years later she was dubbed "one of the most exquisitely gifted artists working today in children's portraits" by an arts magazine in their city. She paints while the kids are in school and still gets to experience all the joys and trials of being a stay-at-home mom.

What I see happening again and again is that when a woman makes a conscious decision to put her marriage and family first, and yes, even to submit to her husband, God honors that decision by giving her work that delights her without putting her mental health or her family at risk. Every family, every neighborhood, has these success stories—and you can be one of them too. If you're a stay-at-home mom now, that doesn't mean things won't change later. And if they do, God will help you prepare for it.

Some women, of course, consciously choose to be full-time, stay-at-home moms. My stepdaughter Julie made that choice for her twin daughters for seven years—and turned it into an art form. I suppose I'm writing about that job choice last because I can't even visit it without getting tears in my eyes. I'm very grateful that I was at home with my boys during their preschool years. I only wish I had also been fully present emotionally rather than wondering what career opportunities the future held for me. I wish I had fully understood that I already had a job, the most important one imaginable.

My heart goes out to stay-at-home moms, because I know how difficult it can be to feel significant in the midst of runny noses and spilled milk. But when your significance comes from God and him alone, you will feel him smiling over you through every hectic day. A woman in the home is not only preserving her family, she's preserving our culture as she oversees the inner domains of husband, children, and home. There simply isn't any work we can choose that can demand more of us, nor deliver more benefits.

The woman in the home is also the embodiment of biblical womanhood. In Titus 2:4–5 older women are encouraged to "train the younger women to love their husbands and children, to be self-controlled and pure, to be busy at home...." In the Proverbs 31 woman we find a wonderful prototype for a woman who was engaged in productive and satisfying work while always keeping her main focus and her heart at home.

In 1 Timothy 5:9–10, Paul writes to Timothy about the widow who is deserving of help, being one who "has been faithful to her husband, and is well known for her good deeds, such as bringing up children, showing hospitality, washing the feet of the saints, helping those in trouble and devoting herself to all kinds of good deeds." This is a beautiful picture of the kind of work God designs for women—the work that will bring them the most joy at the end of the day. And it's all work that is centered around the home.

It was after my children were grown that I answered God's call to go home. I wrote extensively about that experience in my book *It Takes a Home*, but the key points are that God honored my decision, even if it did seem "backwards," and blessed me in ways I could only imagine.

Another complementarian woman has a similar testimony. Priscilla and her husband are childless (not by choice), yet God placed on her heart a desire to quit her high-powered job and simply go home. She did, and at first she wasn't sure why. But soon her home became a gathering place for many neighborhood children. Her availability to neighbors eventually led to a neighborhood Bible study and support group. By shrinking one part of her world and asking her to make home her domain, God expanded her territory to include ministry opportunities unthinkable within her previous schedule. And by doing the work he created for her to do in that season of her life, she blossomed as a nurturing, life-giving woman.

Are you a stay-at-home mom or woman? Be present in the moment. Look around you right now and truly see the power you have to mold lives and create a home that honors God. Blessed are you among women. Hold your head high for, like the Proverbs 31 woman, you are "clothed with strength and dignity" (v. 25).

SPOKEN WITH ALL the authority of a satisfied first-grader whose mommy stayed at home, Caleb said, "Two things that should never be; war and day care." Whether or not we find ourselves in agreement with these evaluations, I submit that the juxtaposition of the two is not as separate as they sound at first hearing. Women who want to work outside the home often have to avail themselves of the provision of day care and this can often result in discord within the home, the church, and the community.

By now, we have repeatedly established the case for a woman to obey only the leadings of her heavenly Father and make decisions according to the inner inclinations of her heart and in mutuality with a husband and her family. If a woman has no interest in looking outside the home for her work, then I commend her and do not even vaguely contend her decision.

However, for the others who do see horizons outside the confines of their home and family, the heavy imprint of patriarchy and the weight of that influence on the interpretations of certain select Scriptures are very effective in hindering them from following that calling.

Flat interpretations of the Bible lead to much dismay, division, and confusion. By "flat" I refer to interpretations of the Word that do not account for culture and custom at the time of writing. Titus 2:5 where Paul encourages young women to be "busy at home" is sometimes teamed up with the classic Proverbs 31 woman in constraining our field of activity to the home.

Paul wrote to a culture where, until the liberating advent of Christianity, women were second-class, largely uneducated citizens. The writer who extolled the virtuous, industrious woman of Proverbs—far from advocating a stay-at-home position—spoke of her expertise in many different areas. Again, hear the explanation that J. Lee Grady gives. "Traditionalists ... would probably not endorse the lifestyle of this woman if they met her on the street.... She was most definitely not a stay-at-home mom in the suburban American sense of the word. Those who use this passage to keep women locked into an exclusively domestic role are misusing Scripture to hold women in a crippling form of religious bondage."[8]

And it was for freedom that Christ set us free. What glorious words those are. The freedom to pursue work outside the home is not part of the feminist agenda—as is often flung about to control a wholesome desire to follow one's dream. Nor does it contribute to the demise and dissolution of the family any more than the march of men carving out a career. Men were the first ones to leave home after the agrarian era ended. Men were the first to be traveling salesmen and, as the tragic picture of Willy Loman in Arthur Miller's powerful play *Death of a Salesman* shows, they often blazed the trail of unfaithfulness in their addiction to both work and women; actions that betrayed and broke up families. A woman going outside the home to work does not demolish the family—the hard hearts of both genders break up homes.

When we do get out there, our contributions are enormous. Rightly applying our gifts, talents, and skills enriches not only the woman, but also the workplace. I am in full concurrence with what Ruth Haley Barton writes in *Equal to the Task*. "It is widely accepted that women and men often bring different leadership styles, values, strengths, and perspectives to the workplace. Some business leaders are more aware than others that the best of what both sexes have to offer is needed for organizations to compete and succeed amid the complexities of today's marketplace."[9]

As complex as the issues are due to outmoded models of women, we must be true to the One who has called us, no matter what the opposition, misunderstanding, or danger. On a recent trip back to my native land, a longtime friend—a male—was reading a book called *She Was Aye Workin'* by Helen Clark and Elizabeth Carnegie. In this recollection of memories of the women who lived in the tenements of Edinburgh and Glasgow, Elaine C. Smith writes in the foreword, "Yes, we know about kings and battles and plagues and fires, but we know so little about how our ancestors really lived—especially the women. Their lives were seen as not mattering as much as men's lives and what went on every day seemed trivial and meaningless ... but, women were aye workin' too."[10] In the hidden confines of the home or under the magnifying glass of the open market, women are always working.

CAN WE AFFORD OUR CHOICES?

EVEN THE RIGHT choices can be wrong if they are made for the wrong reasons. If you've chosen to make home and family your life's work, make sure it's because you hear God's calling as to the sanctity of that choice. Don't make it by default.

If you've chosen to work outside the home, make sure you've selected the kind of work that plays to your strengths as a woman and gives you the opportunity to bring God glory as you approach each task "as working for the Lord" (Col. 3:23). Question your motives, constantly reevaluate your decision, and stay acutely attuned to your family's reactions to your absence. Economic realities exist, but if it's a home in the best neighborhood, private tuition for the children, or an exotic vacation that's sending you out the door, you may not be working for the right reasons. What could you live without in order to spend more waking hours living with your family? What could you give up materially in order to gain spiritually? Every decision we make about work comes with a price. Sometimes the price we pay is simply too high, and no amount of job compensation justifies the sacrifice.

The Old Testament is full of stories about men going to battle. Before the Israelites could enter the Promised Land God told them to go across the Jordan River and clear the land of evil by killing all the men, women, children, and livestock in the cities there. Yet part of the Old Testament law specified that "if a man has recently married he must not be sent to war or have any other duty laid on him" (Deut. 24:5). We no longer live under Old Testament law (thank God), but we've come so far from it that we send many new husbands off to war. And in response to feminist demands, we also send new wives and mothers.

Because my husband and I live in a military town, our newspaper frequently carries photos of soldiers departing for war or, more blessedly, returning home. It's hard to see men going off to fight on foreign soil even though I know God gives them the job of defending our country, homes, and families. What really breaks my heart, however, is seeing a photo of a young mother handing a newborn baby over to a grandparent or husband just before she's deployed. While I applaud her patriotism, the job choice she made carries a price that is simply too high. The sacrifice for her and for her child is far greater than should be required.

The legacy of women in the military is one of pride and honor, but the more recent practice of sending them to the front lines to appease the feminists is a desecration of biblical mandates. And no one seems to care.

"The fog of war and a doggedly sex-neutral, politically correct Pentagon have apparently contributed to the curious phenomenon that female GI deaths in today's combat zones have garnered a minimum of public and press attention," a recent report stated.[11] In addition to the casualties are the infidelities, pregnancies, degrading housing situations, and sacrifice of femininity that can naturally come from placing women in predominately male arenas.

A "sex scandal" at the U.S. Air Force Academy concerning the alleged sexual harassment of female cadets motivated my friend Lea Ann to write a letter to the editor of our paper. "Why have we allowed women in the military academies in the first place?" she writes. "Women are fashioned to give life, not take it.... Our military has been handicapped and weakened by the presence of women just as our families have been handicapped and weakened by the absence of women fulfilling their nurturing roles."

It's not politically correct to say so, but isn't there some truth in what Lea Ann says? For every Jessica Lynch who bravely declares, "I'm an American soldier too," there are many women serving in Iraq who say as one did, "I just want to go home, hug my kids, and take a shower."

Our choices have consequences. Most women who work outside the home may not be handing their newborns over to a relative so they can engage in battle, but who are they handing them over to, and for what reason? Try as they might, feminists cannot fund nor construct a study that disputes the immutable fact that a child under three desperately needs to bond with his or her mother. If he or she is left in day care from dawn till dusk day after day, something precious is irrevocably lost.

Women must be made aware of another price they may pay. If you recall from those days of

Adam and Eve after the fall, God gave a curse to men regarding work, saying "cursed is the ground because of you.... It will produce thorns and thistles" (Gen. 3:17–18). He gave a curse to woman regarding childbirth and the relationship with her husband, saying, "I will greatly increase your pains in childbearing.... Your desire will be for your husband, and he will rule over you" (Gen. 3:16).

The reason many women who work outside the home feel caught in an unending cycle of feeling guilty when they are home about what's not being done at work, and guilty when they are at work about what's not being done at home, is that they are suffering under a double curse. No wonder they fall into bed too exhausted to turn out the light, only to toss and turn restlessly most of the night. It's a high price to pay.

So what are your current choices about work? What price are you paying? What benefits are you gleaning? If you don't ask yourself those questions at least once a week, you aren't being a good steward of the life God has given you to live.

I had a wake-up call about my own choices not long ago. After writing several books that were only moderately successful I found myself questioning my calling. Why, I wondered, when I knew God had directed my writing, hadn't my books been wildly and widely received? I shared my disappointment with a wise friend of ours. Later he called me with one insightful question, "Are you happy with your life now?"

"Yes!" I answered readily. "I love being free to schedule my own work times and to accept or decline assignments. I love being home during the day to see the birds at my window and the cats snoozing in the sunshine. I love being able to prepare dinner for Jim and being free to visit grandkids. I'm glad I can be available to friends and neighbors when they need me."

"Well," he continued. "If you were a world-famous author, don't you think that would change? Would you really want to travel all the time?" Suddenly, what I had seen as disappointing I now saw as God's protection of the life he had given me to live, and I was extremely grateful.

When I questioned my work choices I fell into one of Satan's best traps. He loves to get us to compare ourselves to others and/or to conform our choices to look more like someone else's. But if we do that, we aren't living the authentic lives we were designed to live. Be on guard against Satan's tricks as you make your choices about work.

A proverb says, "What you are is God's gift to you. What you do with yourself is your gift to God." As Rick Warren reminds us in *The Purpose-Driven Life*, "In heaven we are going to serve God forever. Right now, we can prepare for that eternal service by practicing on earth ... We're getting ready for eternal responsibilities and rewards."[12] The choices we make here truly can have long-lasting significance, for us and for our families.

THE CHOICE IS not whether to work at all, but where we will work—at home or outside the home. Prayer, peace, and confidence will earmark the choice we make. Then we must ask ourselves, "Can I afford not to follow my heart?"

If the decision is to stay at home, then we must be sure that it is the seat of our affections. If we are doing it from any other motive, the outcome will be less than healthy. A new friend of mine who has young children recently gave up her well-paying career to be at home and available for her family—opting to live in a more modest home so that her husband's salary would suffice. My daughter did the same several years ago, choosing to leave a job that paid as much as her husband's, so cutting their income in half. She has since reentered the workforce now that her children are older.

That is what I did. When I first arrived in this country from Scotland with my husband and three little children, people often asked what I did. Those were the days when women were streaming out of the home in order to feel productive and significant. I felt both of these in good measure as a full-time mother. When the questioner learned I was a nurse by profession, her enthusiastic rejoinder was that nurses were really needed out there. My answer was always, "The world will find plenty of nurses, but my children have only one mother." End of conversation.

However, as much as I reveled in working at home with my children, homemaking, and volunteering at their schools, the day came when I wanted to spread my wings. As well as sharing and conferring with my husband and family when I first considered picking up my career again, I went to consult with every working mother I knew to glean from their experience and assimilate their advice. I wanted to be sure that their families were surviving the absence of mom. In other words, is the cookie jar still full and the bread still made from scratch?

Those who do work outside the home come in two categories: those who really want to and those who feel pressured to due to finances. Single women simply must bring in an income. Women with families make their decision based on various factors: whether her husband is willing and/or able to assume the homemaker role, if they can afford the cost of baby-sitting or day care (or if grandparents are available—they don't usually charge as they consider being a part of those precious little lives as payment enough), whether working is worth the additional cost of gas and running another car. For all women trying to make ends meet, solutions sometimes involve working part-time, starting a home-based business, carpooling, and/or trading services (like baby-sitting or housecleaning) with another working mom.

When the decision to work outside the home is made, life for a family is changed. The dynamics that occur when a mother goes to work outside the home are considerable, and the cost for any woman to leave the cloistered safety of her own home is complex. Many layers must be peeled off and examined. Beyond the money issues are the seismic shifts that occur when the matriarch leaves the house for over eight hours a day. As well as determining who now walks the cooped-up pooch, a hundred hitherto unconsidered situations scream for attention, such as laundry, vacuuming, and food preparation. Will a single woman outsource the tasks? Will a married woman recruit the help of husband and children?

All the above points beg for consideration as to cost in time, money, and energy. Equally, we must consider the cost of not following our hearts. If we charge out of the home against our better judgment, then the family may well suffer but we, the women, will chafe under the yoke of guilt and remorse for a long time. We blame ourselves for everything that goes wrong in the family—being the adept travel agents we are for extended trips to the land of guilt. A family in trouble is the result of much more complex causes than the event of a mom going out to work.

The cost is equally high if we do not develop our talents. What we have is a gift from God and is to be used at his direction—not neglected or ignored. To quell the passion and purpose that bubbles up in us results in frustration and resentment that may well manifest in fraught family relationships.

The cardinal consideration as we count the cost of our decision is "What does my Father want?" No dogma, tradition, or patriarchy can be weighed on the same scales as heaven's criterion. As we listen for the still small voice of direction from him, we will not flatten under the hurricane of traditionalist hectoring; we will stand up straight in the earthquake of criticism from friends and family and even the fire of religion restrictions will not weaken our resolve.

The price may be high no matter what we choose. The woman who leaves her home every morning to find her satisfaction is to be commended no more or less than the industrious woman working at home. Each is doing it as unto the Lord (Col. 3:17). We have no right to rate one as better than the other. We choose freely in concert with the Spirit of God as our guide, and we count the cost of that choice in the light, love, and liberty of his approval. If those are our benchmarks, no one suffers loss.

Reconciling Our Differences

While we may have differing premises on the traditional models of a woman and her work, we agree that good, satisfying work is a God-given thing and that all women work—period. We are both strong advocates for carefully considering all aspects when making work decisions. We support women in whatever choice they make.

Chapter 5

Following Our Calling

The Ministry of a Woman

Preach the Gospel at all times and when necessary use words.
—Saint Francis of Assisi

What Is a Woman's Role Inside the Church?

ALICE

A GANGLY, SCOTTISH Presbyterian minister I once knew said, "I dinna think that God meant women to be in the pulpit for their voices dinna carry far enough!" Well, it would appear that he had not yet become acquainted with microphones and PA systems. He was, perhaps, more familiar with the sentiments of his predecessor and fellow Scot, John Knox, who is credited with heralding the trumpet against "the monstrous regiment of women."

Perhaps if we consider the word *serve* in place of ministry, we would silence the controversy over who is eligible to minister. Seen as a serving rather than a ruling role, ministry would mean following in the footsteps of Jesus who came to wash feet: to be the least, not the greatest. However, such a simple, albeit profound, explanation will do little to assuage those who insist that sound doctrine dictates a limited role for women within the church. By the church we mean the congregation, the organized system or denomination—not the universal body of Christ, which is an organism, not an organization.

In the organization, a woman is traditionally relegated to roles that put her under the leadership of men rather than being allowed to be a leader herself. This argument usually begins with the citation of I Timothy 2:8–15. This text is a classic case of interpreting male and female roles according to blue and pink hermeneutics. Just to provoke thought around one particular part of this letter to Timothy, look at Paul's injunction that men in every place lift up holy hands without anger or argument; it comes in the same breath as his forbidding women to teach or have authority over a man. How many of us even know that this injunction to men exists? How many of us know the other restriction? We know the second all too well. "The text addressed to men about what to do with their hands has never been enforced in any church I have ever attended," elaborates Christiane Carlson-Theis on this text in an issue of *Priscilla Papers*. "It certainly has not been used to define a universal 'male identity' as 'those-whose-hands-are-always-lifted-in-prayer.' In contrast, the text limiting women's teaching and authority over men has become a central, defining text for the very meaning of womanhood as 'those-who-may-not-teach-or-have-authority-over-men.'"[1]

When we select certain Scriptures to support the case of women's subjugation—and they do appear to be there at first glance—we are in danger of taking selected verses to define dogma while disregarding the overall principles of God's Word and the overwhelming evidence that women have equal rights in his original plan. When we look at the creation account it is clear that God created humankind equally competent, creative, and responsible because both male and female bear the imprint of God himself. It would take the subsequent fall from grace of both genders to set the stage for the centuries of fear, misunderstanding, and competition that divide their roles. They were created for mutuality and oneness, not subjugation and separateness.

Then came Jesus, the great emancipator of women in both his life and death. The ministry that he gave to the woman at the well—despised not only because of her ethnicity, but also because she was a woman and a frequently married one at that—was to tell a town that the Messiah had come. He did not disregard her gender and assign a male to herald the good news. To the women who met him at the empty tomb, he assigned the task of telling the male disciples that he had risen from the dead. These are both significant and persuasive enough examples as to hush the protests that women should not be given the job of either preaching the gospel or preaching to men. Even if we had neither of these examples, his death and resurrection dealt the final blow to the dark, hostile, and hurtful separation of the genders. Galatians 3:28, the charter of our new covenant, boldly declares that "there is neither Jew nor Greek, slave nor free, male nor female, for you are all one in Christ Jesus."

It is that *in* position that seals our credentials. His life given to us who believe, whether male or female, renders null and void the need to decide responsibilities and roles by gender. Indeed that Life alone ministers with authority, for we can do nothing in and of ourselves. The new covenant supersedes all assignments based on gender. We are compelled to interpret Scriptures, such as the one in Timothy, in the light of their historical context—their import to the culture of the time—and not as forever limiting and binding. Remember, Paul was transitioning from a culture where a man—and no doubt he, a self-proclaimed Jew of Jews—thanked God every morning that he was created a man, not a dog or a woman. Nonetheless, the apostle Paul had several female coworkers.

A woman's role in the church should be limited only by her talents and abilities, not her gender. As her male counterpart is never disqualified because of gender, neither should she be. She should have the opportunity to preach (and to be ordained, if that is the requirement of the denomination), teach, administer, or lead according to her calling and character. A woman's talents, which are considerable, are so often wasted and missed by denying her the use of her God-given rights. These are lost to the church by the edict of patriarchy, pride, and presumption.

ALICE

THE PRAISE AND worship song "Shout to the North" beautifully illustrates the importance of each gender in the life of the church. The first stanza calls "men of faith" to sing of the King. In our church just the men sing this stanza, their deep voices thundering through the sanctuary powerfully. The second stanza is sung by only the women in the congregation. "Women of the truth" are called to sing to broken hearts. The women's voices are as smooth and clear as water rolling over rocks in a stream, filling every void with peace and joy. Yet it's not until the third stanza, when the men and women combine their powerful and melodious voices, that the song feels complete. "Rise up church with broken wings," and the sanctuary resounds with praise to the Lord who calls his church to unity and action. It is a beautiful statement to the fact that it takes both men and women, offering their unique gifts in unity, to bring harmony and beauty to the church.[2]

How disappointed I was when we visited a "gender neutral" church, and I saw this favorite

NANCY

song of mine printed in the bulletin, revised to a more "politically correct" version. Everyone sang all the lyrics. Gone were the men of faith. "All of faith rise up and sing," I read on the song sheet. Even the "women of the truth" had become the "people of the truth."

Now of course men don't have an exclusive claim to faith any more than women can claim to be the only gender capable of representing the truth. But the point of the song as originally written is that when men provide their part of the worship experience and women provide theirs, their unique gifts can be recognized and appreciated. And when these unique gifts are combined, the result is awesome!

Every woman who is a believer in Jesus Christ has been endowed with at least one spiritual gift. Beyond that, as a human being created in the image of God she no doubt has many other skills and talents that God expects her to use to his glory. I believe she is called to bring all of her gifts inside the walls of the church, but to use them with discernment so as to complete the men God has called to lead the church, not compete with them. This doesn't mean a woman is powerless to influence the work of the body of Christ. Just as a godly husband takes the advice of his wife into consideration in all his decisionmaking, the godly elders and pastors of the church are wise to solicit and adopt the opinions and counsel of godly women. It is our responsibility as women to offer both respectfully.

Our society is not always comfortable with the difference between secular and Christian models of leadership. As a woman who managed a department of writers and artists within a major corporation and oversaw a multimillion-dollar budget, I was surprised as a reborn believer by the idea that women shouldn't assume similar roles of leadership in the church. And yet the more I studied what the Bible says about God's assigned roles, the more I realized that I would need a different style of leadership if I was to serve his church the way he asks me to serve. My leadership would come more from prayerfully filling the roles God asks me to fill than from being in charge.

Writing in their book *Leadership for Women in the Church*, Susan Hunt and Peggy Hutcheson note the difference between a management style of leadership and leadership that is influence based: the latter is second nature for many women—and is extremely effective. "When women have a vision of what might be anywhere in God's world, whether it is in their homes, their businesses, or their churches, they can contribute and lead in accomplishing this vision," they write. "They are no longer constrained by the view that leading is equal to seeking positions of authority or power. Churches are then free to tap the gifts of all their members more directly, without violating doctrine or challenging tradition."[3]

What are the biblical roles of women for ministry within the church? Primarily to teach and encourage younger women, teach and nurture children, provide wisdom and guidance to men in positions of leadership, and serve as deacons when this office is defined as service to the church body. This sounds limiting to some, but it is extremely liberating and exhilarating to those who are brave enough, and secure enough in their identity in Christ, to give it a try.

Titus 2:3–5 reads, "Likewise, teach the older women to be reverent in the way they live, not to be slanderers or addicted to much wine, but to teach what is good. Then they can train the younger women to love their husbands and children, to be self-controlled and pure, to be busy at home, to be kind, and to be subject to their husbands, so that no one will malign the word of God."

Doesn't that sound like enough to do? Women have an inordinate amount of work to accomplish in the world. Whether they are employed outside the home or serving as home managers all day, they are often overworked and underappreciated. Is it just possible that, knowing women would naturally carry most of the load of rearing children, running a home, and sustaining the culture, God thought they deserved a break when they went to church? Finally, we have a place of sanctuary where someone else is responsible—and held accountable; a place where we can rest under the protection God put in place for us. Why can't women be content in that and find restoration and peace in God's plan?

Although I've held several positions of leadership in my life, with all the responsibility and stress such positions entail, I feel most fulfilled and valued when I'm exercising the kind of self-discipline described in Titus 2. It's gratifying to pass along what I've learned about being a mother and a wife, including the mistakes I've made and the forgiveness I've received, to women younger in years or younger in the faith.

Those who think following the traditional roles of service for women in a church means subjecting themselves to decades of pouring orange juice into paper cups and passing out Vanilla Wafers just don't understand the creative power of God—the power that gifts us with the ability to shape lives and pass on a legacy of wisdom and encouragement. And by the way, if we don't do these things, who will? Could the obvious answer to that question be the reason we were asked to do them?

The primary verses debated in terms of women's roles in the church are I Timothy 2:12, where Paul writes, "I do not permit a woman to teach or to have authority over a man; she must be silent," and I Corinthians 14:34–35, where he writes, "Women should remain silent in the churches. They are not allowed to speak, but must be in submission.... If they want to inquire about something, they should ask their own husbands at home; for it is disgraceful for a woman to speak in the church."

I've read and studied many different theological and hermeneutical interpretations of these two Scripture verses, but the interpretations that directly influence the choices I make are the ones the Holy Spirit has revealed to me in truth and sealed in my heart in love. These are the interpretations I most want to share.

Let's look at the 1 Timothy verse first. The direction God breathed into Scripture through his servant Paul is that women should not "teach or have authority over a man." Not that they shouldn't teach or have authority within the church—for of course they must bear witness in both areas—but that they should not rule over men, meaning they should not be in the authoritative positions of pastor, teacher, or elder. The reasons Paul gives for this mandate in 1 Timothy 2:13–14 are not easily endorsed by all but are clearly stated nevertheless: 1) because Adam was created first and 2) because Eve was deceived.

We can't begin to reason as God reasons, but my understanding as to why he chose to limit the teaching and authority of women in this way is because he asks the men to step up and fill positions of leadership in the church. As has already been established, men and women are equally valued by God. Certainly he could have chosen to ask women to lead and men to follow them. The immutable truth is that he didn't make that choice. Rather he asked women to master certain areas of the life of the church and assigned men to other tasks. This is clearly stated in 1 Timothy 3:2 where Paul talks about the elder being the "husband of but one wife." God wants men to assume the positions of responsibility and leadership he has given them, and as added insurance to make sure that happens, he asks women to direct their attention elsewhere.

Can a woman teach in church? Of course she can. She can freely teach other women and children.

She can also teach adults of all ages and both genders as long as she is not doing so with a domineering spirit, but under the authority of a male teacher or pastor. Why is that necessary? Because it respects God's created order and his inerrant Word, both of which firmly establish the importance of women's contributions as well.

What about the silence factor addressed in 1 Corinthians 14? Anyone who lingers for coffee after a Sunday morning service knows that women are not known for staying silent in church. The roar of the conversation, mostly female, escalates until the aisles are clear or the first notes of a song announcing the start of the next service waft through the air. On the question of silence, liberal and conservative scholars seem to agree. In 1 Corinthians 14 Paul was writing to a church in Corinth that was disorderly and out of control. He wanted to encourage the churchgoers to do what was proper and orderly; according to Paul, that included women praying or prophesying in church with an attitude of submission and not speaking up during periods of instruction.

So how does a godly woman translate Paul's statement into a godly attitude today? Primarily, it means she should not serve in a preaching capacity where men are present. Moreover, as believers we are all called to guard our tongues, to say only those things that are edifying to others, and to abstain from gossip. I work at following those scriptural guidelines at all times, but because of Paul's instruction to the Corinthians, I'm especially aware of them at church. And because I believe in God's awesome, functioning plan of submission, I'm perfectly content with taking my questions and problems about the church to my husband first, asking him to answer my questions, represent me to the elders or the pastor, or send me to them for answers.

Why am I happy with this arrangement? Because God asked me to do it that way, then gave me a husband with a listening heart and an obedient spirit. Because it honors God and my husband and demonstrates my respect for both. And because it works. I realize other women may not have listening, obedient husbands. Nonetheless, they will also benefit from following God's plan if they stay close to God in prayer.

Writing in *Women in Ministry, Four Views*, contributor Robert D. Culver reminds us that the church has "innumerable avenues of service, social expression, and of Christian witness for women within the biblical limits of the tradition of male authority. This has always been the case and remains true to the present."[4] It is the wise pastor and board of elders who tap into this incredible resource in creative yet biblical ways.

But what about the woman who feels undeniably called to a full-time career as an ordained pastor? Believing that we truly "can do everything through him who gives me strength" (Phil. 4:13), it's hard to suggest that such a woman should deny this calling. But the questions she needs to ask herself are: "Did I hear God correctly in terms of how I am to serve?" and "What is the basic reason ordination is so important to me?"

Those who have heard Anne Graham Lotz speak say there is no question but that she is an anointed evangelist. Her father, Billy Graham, has reportedly declared her the best preacher in the family. I don't know exactly how Mrs. Lotz views her role as preacher and teacher, but I've read enough of her writing to know that her heart attitude is to bring glory to God in everything she does. God told her to share the gospel to all who would listen, so she does just that. Still, she chooses not to be ordained and has no problem operating under the lordship of Jesus Christ and the headship of her father and her husband.

It does come back to heart attitude, doesn't it? In one sense all believers are ordained by the Holy Spirit to use the gifts we have been given, so ordination in itself is not the issue. Certainly I can understand why a woman who has devoted years to the study of theology, a woman who feels a strong calling on her heart to devote her life to full-time ministry, would desire the formal sanction and affirmation that ordination carries in the eyes of the secular world and the organized church. But the ordination itself does not mean she is to serve outside of the roles of ministry God has designed for women. The question becomes whether she deems such formal ordination by a denomination as affirmation of her call to serve in the areas of ministry in which God has asked women to serve or as an outward sign that she has power over men—or that she is qualified to fulfill even the roles of ministry that the Bible clearly assigns to men. The answer lies somewhere between her heart and God's.

One scholar versed in gender roles termed the power-seeking type of ordination "the forbidden fruit" of evangelical feminism. In other words, because it may represent the one thing God asks women not to do, teach and rule over men in the church, it becomes the ultimate goal of those who have been deceived to believe a call to ministry is automatically a call to rule. A woman with such a calling should be encouraged to interpret her call in accordance with Scripture rather than search for ways to reinterpret the Bible to justify her feelings about leadership. Our feelings can deceive us, but the Word of God will not.

It's hard for us to hold fast to what we believe is true when someone we love and admire has heard a different call and taken a different path. During the same years that I was learning the essence of biblical womanhood, my stepdaughter Joelle was in seminary preparing to be an ordained minister in the Presbyterian church. Not only was she doing well in school, she won the top preaching award just before graduating with honors!

I went to the Lord often to ask him how I was to reconcile what he was teaching me about the role of women in the church with my pride, love, and admiration for Joelle. One day as I was praying, I heard his answer. "She belongs to me," he said. "I'll take care of her spiritual journey. It doesn't need to concern you."

Hearing the admonition to relax made it much easier to attend Joelle's graduation from seminary and her subsequent ordination and to truly be proud of her individual achievements and pleased with God's calling on her life. And true to his promise, I have seen God leading her in the direction he wants her to go. Whereas her first position as a pastor in a church was more intense, she's now working part-time as pastor of children's ministry in a large church near her home.

The change came as a result of a move that Joelle and her family made so that her husband, Scott, could pursue a job opportunity that would enable him to be a better provider for their family. He had moved several times in support of Joelle's calling, so she felt it was her turn to give up her job and move where he needed to go. I clearly see that God honored her decision and her submission—so much so that he went before her to prepare the way. Shortly after the move, Joelle walked into a neighborhood church seeking day care for our grandson Charlie. Soon she learned that the church was looking for a part-time, female, ordained pastor for the children's ministry. She applied and got the job. God is in the details, and he's working all things together for good in her life.

Part of maturing in the Lord is realizing that he calls us differently. Another song echoes in my heart whenever I think of my own submission to God regarding the role he has asked me to play in the church. "We bring the sacrifice of praise into the house of the Lord," it proclaims.[5] My submission to the will of God as expressed in his Holy Word is the sacrifice I bring, and I lay everything

NANCY

that would distract me from obeying him on the altar. My need to be in charge is there. My desire to show men that women can do everything men can do is there. My tendency to want to fix things my way is there. And as I walk away to serve him, my heart cry is like that of Mary the mother of Jesus who said, "'I am the Lord's servant.' ... 'May it be to me as you have said'" (Luke 1:38).

How Does She Minister Outside the Church?

ALICE

TWENTY YEARS AGO I, with a team of women teachers, charged up and down the country of my native land of Britain ministering the Word of God. While the Church of England Synod debated the eligibility of women to serve as priests, we held our first *Women of the Word* International Conference in a nearby city. Hundreds of women from across the country, and the world, celebrated their inheritance in Christ. God gave me the heart, the opportunity, and the ability to teach women who they were in Christ—and that message set hundreds free to tell others that God has no glass ceiling and has great and glorious purposes for women everywhere. All this we did outside the organized church as we obeyed the mandate that God had given to us. It is essential that women come to the place of freedom and confidence that persuades them that it is more important to obey God rather than man.

In order for women to feel free to minister in or out of the organized church, it is helpful to consider what the early church really looked like in order to understand the prevailing customs and the culture of the day. The believers met primarily in homes. They had no Scriptures, as we know them today, and no local bookstore from which to shop for the latest leather-bound edition of the Bible. All that existed of God's record to humankind was the Torah—which was a closed book to women for they were denied formal study of Holy Writ, formal education being the domain of the male. The first inspired writings that the nascent church had were the letters of Paul that we know as the Epistles. These were simply that: letters passed on from gathering to gathering (no copy machines either!). Since they came some fifty to sixty years after Jesus Christ had died, an entire generation of believers would have died without ever having read the Word as we know it. It is interesting to reflect that the entire Bible that we use to establish our dogmas is a book that our first brothers and sisters in the faith never read.

If we are willing to explore the context of the Scriptures with intellectual honesty, it will help us come to understand what constitutes the continuing dilemma regarding the role of women in the body of Christ. "We recognize the need to find out something about the Assyrians or Babylonians to understand what the prophets proclaimed, but we often fail to ask about the historical context into which the New Testament authors wrote,"

writes James R. Payton Jr., professor of history at Redeemer University College in Ancaster, Ontario. "Much of the time, we approach passages in the New Testament almost as if they were written with the twenty-first century in mind. Of course they weren't. One of the things that strikes me about the debate over the roles of women in the church ... is how little attention has been shown to the question of the historical context made by the New Testament authors."[6]

Women have long beaten the system in finding their way to the foreign mission field. Although the protocol and procedures are quite different in our changing global environment from what many of our heroines knew in other centuries, nonetheless these courageous women served as models of inspiration, courage, and fortitude. The China Inland Mission rejected Gladys Aylward, but she went independently to that great land and in 1938 led a group of orphans on a perilous journey to Siam that became the theme of the movie, *The Inn of the Sixth Happiness*. Then there was Lottie Moon who sailed for China in 1870 and spent over forty years there. Even today, women still return from a productive mission field often to find they are still not eligible to serve on their church board.

If we are contented ministering only outside the building and in unofficial, relegated roles, then that is commendable. Godliness with contentment is great gain. However, if we know deep down that we are restricted due to patriarchy, hermeneutics, or hierarchy, trust the God who has

ALICE

called and equipped us—he will make a way. Stand firm, stand sure, and stand sweet. Let God's gentleness make us great.

No matter how wronged we may feel when unable to access "official" ministry, we must make sure that bitterness does not choke the channels we presently have at our disposal. Let us not waste time and energy contesting the disparities at the expense of doing what is at hand to do. Opportunities to teach women's Bible classes, to volunteer at a pregnancy clinic that provides alternatives to abortion, to teach a group of junior high girls in your basement after school, to teach Sunday school in church always exist.[†] Remember, the world is our field; it is fertile for seed to be sown into and ripe from which to gather a harvest where others have labored.

NANCY

NOT A REALM of family or community life can't be improved and enhanced by the involvement and ministry of women. It is women who have traditionally brought culture and beauty to society, and they continue to be life-givers in all areas of commercial and community life.

When I think back through my own personal ministries I realize that I didn't even always think of them as ministries at the time. Is it a ministry

---

[†] I have often wondered about the presence of boys in such a gathering—just when do they become male? Under the present guidelines, do they not also constitute the category of "teaching men"?

if you offer to drive an extra carpool because your neighbor looks tired? Sure it is. Is it glorifying to God if you put your work aside in order to counsel a harried coworker? Without a doubt. Not only that, but I found that whenever I put people first in my job, God would faithfully redeem any time I spent.

Sometimes our ministries are more clearly defined, to be sure. Maybe you volunteer on a community board or serve as a hospice counselor. Maybe you help out at your child's school or lead a Bible study at a nursing home. Whatever you are doing is a ministry when you do it as to the Lord.

The challenge is often not how can I minister, but rather which ministries should I choose and how do I know when I've chosen too many at once? A true assessment of your spiritual gifts, as well as your talents and skills, is a good place to start. Our time is limited, so we want to invest it where it will make the most difference for this world and for the kingdom. A wise woman who wants to maximize her personal ministry opens her heart to God's leading in prayer. She takes her assignments from and answers first to him, then to her husband if she is married. She learns how to spend her time wisely and to say no when she needs to—but her options for ministry are boundless.

Having served several different community organizations and parachurch ministries, I'm realizing the primary ministry of my life now is something I've come to term the "ministry of availability." Have you noticed how many people really aren't available anymore? Jobs and family responsibilities make it impossible for them to change plans at a minute's notice. But as an empty nester working at home, God has allowed me the opportunity to have an expansive ministry of availability in this season of my life. I just had to realize it was a ministry so I could stop thinking of it as a series of interruptions in my day.

Right now being available means I'm free to take a dear friend in her eighties who is diagnosed with a malignant brain tumor to the hospital to visit her special fellow who is recovering from surgery. Through them I am seeing both a glimpse of the difficulty of aging and a testimony to the beauty of love at any age. As with most ministries, the benefits far outweigh the effort.

How does a woman who is secure in Christ minister outside of the church? She does it exuberantly, lavishly, creatively, and gloriously! Find out what God's doing and join him in it. He wants to use you.

What Does God Expect?

GOD EXPECTS US to be faithful to use the talents and gifts with which he has entrusted us. If we have had only meager substances and circumstances such as hay or stubble with which to work, then we are still accountable for that stewardship. If we have been gifted more generously with what would constitute silver and gold, then only if it is used to build on the finished work of the cross, will it have any lasting value.

That foundation that the apostle Paul referred to in his writings is none other than the person of the Lord Jesus Christ. The foundation of our life's work is in him who is our source and substance, and it continues to grow productively only in him, the Alpha and Omega. When he was on earth, Jesus said that he did only the things that the Father told him. If we were to do likewise, that would certainly take care of all the thrashing around we sometimes engage in trying to find God's will for our lives. How freeing it is for women to understand that we can do nothing without him—in contrast to feeling we can do nothing without the permission of men. Above all, let all be done in love for nothing else will stand the test of time. Everything else will pass away—all the great gifts, the spectacular ministries, the accolades and acknowledgements.

The criteria by which we are judged as women will be no different from what is expected of all believers. That in itself should tell us that in our earthly lives no standard separates females and males. The love that we operate in will primarily be manifest in freedom from fear. So, if fear hampers our ability to run free as an equal in the church, then we have not yet been perfected in the love that banishes trepidation, releases potential, and pleases all our Father's expectations. He has paid the ultimate price for us, so let us thank him by taking advantage of that bounty from which he has given so generously.

NANCY

FEW OF US begin a new job feeling completely competent in every way. After I received a promotion at work a friend and coworker left something on my desk that helped me put all my self-doubts into perspective. It was a beautiful calligraphy rendition of Micah 6:8: "And what does the LORD require of you? To act justly and to love mercy and to walk humbly with your God." That really is what he expects, isn't it? That, and to love the Lord our God with all our heart, soul, and mind and our neighbors as ourselves. Such simple requirements that redirect every aspect of life.

So how does this apply to what God expects of us as women in ministry? I believe we can't succeed in ministry in or out of the church until we first stop to listen to the truth he is speaking into our hearts. We do that through quiet time with him in Bible study and prayer, through the people he sends into our lives, and through the circumstances he allows to surround us.

Sincerely ask the Lord how he wants you to respond to his guidelines regarding women in the church. What sacrifices is he asking you to bring to his altar? What silence is he asking you to maintain? Can you be comfortable forgoing earthly power knowing that you have access to his almighty power? God expects you to ask yourself these questions and listen for his answers.

I also think God expects us to stand firm in our faith, to fully believe what he has told us is true, and to act accordingly. We can't truly act justly, show mercy to others, and walk humbly with him unless we are totally aware of the source

NANCY

of the strength we have to do these things. That strength comes only, always from him.

Finally, I believe God expects us to dwell in unity as brothers and sisters in Christ. Women will certainly interpret their calls to ministry in different ways, but we can still love each other unconditionally. I believe God expects no less of us.

RECONCILING OUR DIFFERENCES

Whether a woman pours orange juice or the cup of Communion, we believe she is empowered by Christ alone. She has nothing over which to boast because his blood has bought her and placed her in his body, the true church. Lest we want to break and bruise that body again, we humbly acknowledge that we are but separate parts of a whole that immense and powerful love has built.

We easily agree that the Lord calls women to serve on this earth, even if we disagree about what that ministry is. We not only believe it, we live it; for we are sure he brought us together, a theological "odd couple" of sorts, and gave us simultaneously the desire to share his message of unity and love in the midst of disagreement. As scary as it seemed at times, we could only respond, "Yes, Lord."

Chapter 6

Confronting Hard Questions
Challenging Issues

*The greatest happiness in life is the
conviction that we are loved—
loved for ourselves, or rather,
loved in spite of ourselves.*

—Victor Hugo

CAN A CHRISTIAN BE A FEMINIST?

NANCY

I ANSWER THIS question after much prayer because I realize my answer has the potential for stepping on the toes of several women I love. Yet, I feel I must share how I've reached my convictions. Let's begin with a series of definitions. Secularly speaking, a feminist is defined as one whose beliefs and behaviors are based on feminism. Feminism is defined as 1) belief in the social, political, and economic equality of the sexes and 2) the movement organized around these beliefs.

Many Christian women are feminists in terms of defending equal pay for equal work or basic human rights for the oppressed women of the world. But once they begin to apply "equality" to their roles as a member of the church or a wife in the home—i.e., once they confuse being equally valued in God's eyes with the created differences and roles God ordained for biblical womanhood and manhood—the personal and societal ramifications can be extremely severe. Such feminists within the faith are known as evangelical feminists, biblical feminists, or egalitarians.

Throughout the chapters of this book the debate is the same: Are we following the inerrant Word of God as inspired by him, or are we reinterpreting it to suit our personal or cultural prejudices and desires? So it is with biblical feminism.

An excellent book by Mary A. Kassian titled *The Feminist Gospel: The Movement to Unite Feminism with the Church* gives a detailed history of the origin of the feminist movement and its eventual entrée into the life of the church. Two female theologians, Letty Russell and Rosemary Radford Ruether, launched a powerful effort in the early '70s to establish what they termed "feminist liberation theology." Kassian details their successes and failures but points out that a major flaw was that "instead of deciding what liberation and freedom meant, according to the Bible, they interpreted the Bible according to their preconceived definitions of those terms."[1]

The aftershocks of this perhaps well-intended but misguided movement are still being felt in the church today as local congregations and entire denominations debate, or divide over, issues relating to the role of women in the church, particularly the ordination of women. At the bottom of the slippery slope (and for the sake of unity in the body I can only hope we're at least near the bottom) many conservative Christians feel the ordination of women has led to the next logical ramification: the ordination of homosexuals. The Council for Biblical Manhood and Womanhood Web site states, "To us it is increasingly and painfully clear that biblical feminism is an unwitting partner in unraveling the fabric of complementary manhood and womanhood that provides the foundation not only for biblical marriage and biblical church order, but also for heterosexuality itself."[2]

I realize these are radical concepts for the egalitarian woman who merely seeks "liberty and justice for all," yet she should be aware of the ramifications of interjecting the tenets of self-serving secular feminism into the roles God established for men and women ... and into his church. In her book *Feminism: Mystique or Mistake?* Diane Passno quite candidly summarizes the problem by saying, "Feminists in their arrogance have replaced the sovereignty of God with the sovereignty of women. God has been rationalized out of existence."[3]

Can a Christian be a femininst? Certainly there are evangelical feminists who have accepted salvation through Jesus Christ and so are unquestionably Christians. However, the Christian woman who fully embraces the biblical instructions given to her gender—as seen in her ability to

NANCY complement men, to nurture, to bring life and sustain culture, and to fulfill the duties in the home and the church that God asks her to fulfill—is the wisest, strongest, most beautiful image of femininity by any definition.

WE WOULD PROBABLY all agree that the word *Christian* describes a believer in Jesus Christ as Savior. A feminist is one who subscribes to the definition of the word *feminism*—a belief in women's rights. Lots of "ism's" sound sinister to me. I looked up this little suffix in the dictionary and found my fears confirmed. Some of the examples—that of making a noun into a state, condition, or belief system—read thus: *mesmerism, gangsterism, defeatism,* and *caffeinism.* The detractors of women's rights have turned the acceptable belief system of *feminism* into a pejorative one. Instead of the word conjuring up a picture of freedom and parity, it now raises the specter of untamed women threatening to destroy the very fabric of society.

Christians are the best-equipped people in society to support equal rights for women; though, sadly, such a belief system does not prevail in Christendom. The absence of this ethos is tragic as well as intellectually and spiritually dishonest for it flagrantly defies Galatians 3:26–28: "You are all sons of God through faith in Christ Jesus, for all of you who were baptized into Christ have clothed yourselves with Christ. There is neither Jew nor

ALICE

Greek, slave nor free, male nor female, for you are all one in Christ Jesus."

To posit a partial equality in the secular arena only—as some do—while shunning parity in the home and church, constitutes a strange half-truth. In preceding chapters, I have referenced the historical, traditional, and cultural constructs that have contributed to the heresy of women's secondary status—the genesis of dissension and discontent. To argue that Betty Freidan's book *The Feminine Mystique* in 1963 launched the women's movement underscores the ignorance behind which many anti-women's rights adherents hide. "The historical origin of evangelical feminism as a 'movement' can be located in the writings of Sarah Grimke, an abolitionist of the 19th century," writes the scholarly Rebecca Merrill Groothuis. "Beginning with Grimke in the 1830s, the evangelical leaders in early American feminism maintained that the Bible had been mistranslated and misinterpreted by men so as to appear to teach the subordination of women as a universal norm ... the women's movement of the 19th century arose in large part from the concerns of Christian women such as Sarah Grimke who began to speak out against slavery, and wound up having to defend their rights as women to speak publicly about anything at all."[4]

Some hold the shallow perspective that past protests by women demanding rights and redresses were more accepted and approved than those of their latter-day counterparts. The establishment certainly did not embrace the first suffragettes; rather they were thrown into prison for their pains. Regrettably, the violence of their own actions—born out of intense frustration—contributed to the disintegration and demise of their dreams. Not until the changes crawled through the legislative process were women allowed to vote state by state. Finally a women's franchise was signed into law in these United States in 1920—nearly one hundred years after the Grimke sisters' efforts.

Vitriolic attacks on patriarchal establishments in general and the male of the species in particular contributed to the collapse of the well-intentioned feminist movement of the '60s, just as violence hurt the cause of their forerunners. Christian women cannot condone violence of any kind. We cannot tolerate teachings that assault the vital quality of life to which we are entitled as daughters of the King of the universe. We must intercept the passing of the cup of Kool-Aid disguised as a thirst-quencher for feminine fulfillment, but which is laced with the lies of legalism. We must be there to replace it with a draft of the life-giving words of freedom that will slake the fiercest thirst. We must protest the theft of our right to speak and be heard in the marketplace of human affairs and have parity with men at work, in the church, and in the home. This is the work of the Christian feminist.

Women longing for a dose of realism (now there is a good *ism*) in our spiritual lives, smarting under the rod of male dominance, search for the softer, gentler side of God. Frequently we find only the light touch of liberal theology that ignores the veracity of the Word of God or the siren goddess of feminism who enfolds us to her false breast. Christian feminism, on the other hand, is only liberal in its lavish supply of love and it is no goddess religion—it is a God-united relationship that satisfies, soothes, and surpasses any counterfeit. It is an invitation to intimacy: to snuggle into the strong, tender arms of our Creator Redeemer's embrace and to go forth stronger ourselves.

Paul R. Smith in his book with the provocative title of *Is It Okay to Call God "Mother"?* puts his finger on the pulse of the feminist question when he writes, "Centuries of assault on the nurturing, maternal, and compassionate images of God have resulted in the virtual abortion of the feminine in much of the church today. This dismemberment and discarding of the feminine in leadership and language is the most pressing theological and social agenda within the American church today."[5]

Failure to embrace a healthy view of feminism has left a gaping hole in our communal life. Its exclusion, rather than its inclusion, is the reason for counterfeits and confused identities. The aversion to the "slippery slope" that the antifeminist camp refers to in its fear of where the feminist movement may lead, is understandable—it is the natural fear of being out of control. The rubric of recovering biblical manhood and womanhood, and others—in their attempt to control the destiny of women—are

ALICE

no match for the God who controls the course of history, who tells the waves where to stop in the march of the tides. To attempt to stop the march of freedom which he purchased for everyone—and cost him everything—is a matter of great gravitas. Christian feminism at its best—full of grace and truth—helps stem the tide of rhetoric and fear.

How Does a Christian Handle Divorce?

NANCY

THERE ARE MANY reasons why a marriage fails, but basically it comes down to the failure of one or both of the married parties to subscribe to God's plan for submission and headship. Perhaps the wife allows her desire to control her husband, a result of the curse in Genesis 3:16, to create tension in the home. Maybe the husband ignores his obligation to love his wife as fervently as Christ loves the church.

Most marriages that die do so by degrees. In October 1971 I had just taken my first husband of three years to the airport to leave for his tour of duty in Vietnam. After tucking my fifteen-month-old son into bed, I collapsed into a yellow armchair my parents had just given us to furnish the little house I would live in while my husband was away. I remember sitting in that chair sobbing. My sister had brought over a large yellow chrysanthemum plant earlier in the day to cheer me up, and it was on the table by the chair.

Another image forever burned into my mind, another promise made.

"I will never allow myself to feel this empty again over love for a man," I said as I stared into that plant. "It hurts too much to love this completely and risk losing it all." And so the emotional wall went up.

My husband came back from Vietnam ten months later, but neither of us was the same—and our marriage was about to undergo radical, negative changes. Looking back, I wonder how critically each of us was wounded by that war. He returned with a compulsion to experience everything life had to offer, good and bad, and never recovered from the need to stay active to dull the pain the war inflicted. I accepted his resulting emotional distance willingly, because it kept me from risking caring as much as I had before. Because we weren't walking with the Lord, the scene was ripe for Satan to make his moves and by 1982 the marriage was over, and our divorce was final. I was a single mom, and my two little boys, then eleven and eight, would only see their reassigned military father on alternate holidays and summer visits.

I truly want to write that every marriage is a holy sacrament and should be maintained no matter what, but because I know all too well the pain of an ailing marriage, I find it hard to make that statement resolutely. I know some marriages must be abandoned to save sanity or life. I also know one person cannot save a marriage alone. But then that's cutting God out of the picture, isn't it?

A friend of mine could be the poster child for sticking with a bad marriage and believing God can work miracles. In spite of what look like impossible circumstances, she continues to walk the path she believes God would have her walk. In an attempt to model faithfulness for her sons, she holds on to the hope for healing. She's a stronger woman than I, and she may be right.

"There is no marital problem so great that God cannot solve it. No marriage—no matter how weak or scarred—need end," wrote Chuck Swindoll.[6] If you are struggling in a difficult marriage right now, hold on to that truth. So many people who have been married for thirty years or more talk about how they weathered the bad times in their marriages. They are so glad they did, for the rewards are many.

I know the pain and grief of a marriage that ends, so when I say divorce should be avoided if at all possible, I know what I'm saying. What those in the midst of the battle don't understand when they take steps toward divorce to escape the pain is that they are simply trading one kind of pain for another, longer lasting one. It's painful to watch your children suffer for years. It's painful to lose all your common history, common memories, and common legacy.

The failure of my first marriage is ancient history. That I can write about it objectively without sobbing is evidence of the grace and mercy of God in my life. I've been fully convicted, and fully forgiven. After I spent seven years as a single mom, God gave me a wonderful Christian husband, and

NANCY

Jim and I have been married since 1988. He is also divorced, and his two daughters shared many of the heartaches my boys knew. But now all four of our kids are married, and we have a host of grandchildren to enjoy and love—"beauty for ashes" to be sure. Neither of us expected to find such happiness in a second marriage, but then we forgot we were serving the God of second chances.

Still, the consequences of our two past divorces continue. God is merciful, but he is just, and he does not remove the consequences of our sinful choices and mistakes. Once Jim and I struggled with which kids would be where on what holiday. Now we have the pain of explaining to our grandchildren why, "Grancy is Dad's mom but Papa isn't his dad," and on and on.

But by the grace of God, we know the consequences of sin don't have to carry forward to all generations of those who know the Lord (Ex. 20:5–6). The pain can end, and forgiveness can free us all. More importantly for the message of this book, God used my past to show me why his wonderful, divine plan of submission and headship, lived out in faith through the love of Jesus Christ, is the best way to build a lasting marriage that honors him.

ALICE

OUR GOD HAS a propensity to construct the most extraordinary events from seemingly foolish elements. He made the earth from chaos and man from the dust of the ground. When he purposed to meld two humans—one a female and the other a male—together in the noble estate of marriage, we could be pardoned for concluding that he may have trumped his highest "foolishness" to date!

Marital bliss seems simply impossible at times as is evidenced by the detritus of divorce, strife, and unhappiness; it is apparent that we cannot conduct this symphony in our own strength. I have recently experienced divorce in my extended family. The pain is paralyzing and the ongoing grief almost too hard to articulate. I recall the dissonance and despair that I often experienced in the tumultuous early years of my own marriage, a pain that wailed, "Why marriage? This is your idea so you must show me how it works!" In the darkest days of my married life, the one hopeful fact to which I clung was that there would be no marriage in heaven.

We were desperate and almost about to give up when Jim and I decided—through gritted teeth and tear-stained faces—that we would throw ourselves on the mercy of God and pretend that the word *divorce* did not exist. It was a turning point in our lives. We continue on a daily journey of submission to Christ in one another and our marriage goes from one degree of glory to the next. I am not prescribing this as a fail-safe formula, but I do hold that a degree of brokenness and tenderheartedness, coupled with a similar commitment, is necessary to prevent fracture of a relationship. Jesus said that God instituted divorce because of hardness of heart (Mark 10:1–9).

When loss of tenderness and tractability tempt us to make choices that lead to divorce, for whatever reason, a woman is still exquisitely loved and cherished for who she is. If we have been bitterly betrayed and our trust shattered, the Savior hurts with us and holds us in the darkness of the night. For whoever has been untrue and has flagrantly violated the marriage vows, the crushing burden of guilt and shame will eventually come rushing in. This is part of the redemptive process as the story of the prodigal details in chapter 15 of Luke's gospel. It is one of the most comforting and awesome stories of forgiveness found in the Bible. For those who wander and then return with a repentant heart, the Father waits and welcomes us home. Oh! The sweetness and strength of that all-encompassing embrace that holds us with not one word of reprimand.

Tucked away in the Old Testament is another amazing story that depicts God's forgiving love. The story of the prophet Hosea and his wife, the whore named Gomer, is a dramatic and riveting reminder of God's pursuing grace. "Go show your love to your wife again, though she is loved by another and is an adulteress. Love her as the LORD loves the Israelites, though they turn to other gods" (Hos. 3:1). Hear how the inimitable preacher and writer T. D. Jakes describes this remarkable reunion in *The Lady, Her Lover, and Her Lord*. "When Hosea finally found Gomer she was in the lowest valley. She was in a deplorable state. She was a mere fragment of what she could have been.... He loved her, and before he would let her go back to what she was, before he would let her be chained to her past, before he would let her be sold back to slavery to obey the whims of every passing stranger in her city, he would redeem her."[7]

We are the redeemed, divorced or not. If the marriage bond is broken lightly, when the woman walks away and abandons her mate and her children without seeming due cause, then her heavenly Daddy will discipline and deal with her heart. I had occasion several years ago to watch the anatomy of a divorce up close and personal—one that my friend initiated and, by her own admission, one for which she had no legitimate reason. I have lost track of her now, for the pleading and admonishing of her friends failed to deter her. What I do know is that the Lord loves her as deeply as he does the woman who is the victim of serious affronts at the hands of an unfaithful husband. The expectation from both the wounded and the perpetrator is that we extend forgiveness and work for reconciliation whenever possible.

I remember a heated debate once in our church small group where it was the cemented opinion of one member that God could not forgive divorce. I have another friend who has remained wedded to a most unbearable man for over forty years and whose reason for not divorcing is, "Because I don't think God would forgive me." With such I plead that they consider the cross and ask which violation the blood of Christ did not wash away. Only pride would conclude that some sins are so flagrant that God does not have the capability to deal with them. Yes, God hates divorce (Mal. 2:16), yet he does not value the institution over the person. Staying in an abusive marriage is not honoring the Christ who is in us.

No matter what the impetus for divorce, the wreckage from the breakup of a family litters everyone's path with betrayal, pain, and grief. While our earthly relationships—the horizontal axis—will register casualties among children, parents, and friends, the vertical axis of the cross that represents our connection to God remains intact, for nothing can separate us from his love. The casualties in relationships are not the direct actions of a punitive God, but simply the logical outcome of life choices. However, a divorced woman does not have to live under condemnation, for there is no condemnation to those who are in Christ Jesus, and that is certainly where the Christian woman has permanent citizenship (Rom. 8:1).

Although hard to believe while the storm is raging, the Father works all things together for good and specializes in clean up after the tsunami of suffering has swept through our families (Rom. 8:28). The temptation throughout our lives is to wallow in "if only." In the case of divorce this is particularly prevalent. "He knew from before the foundation of the world what we would do and say, and knowing it all He loved us," biblical scholar Malcolm Smith wrote. "Now that my failure has been actualized in history, He does not stop loving me. To say 'If only' is to place ourselves with the pagans and their finite gods—gods that can be surprised by the activity of their adherents. God knew what we would do, and fully forgives us through what Christ accomplished at the Cross. Better than that, His love is an infinitely wise love that not only forgives but also actually weaves our mistakes into His plan and turns them for good."[8]

We can trust God with our pain and our past. And we can take advantage of second chances. Many remarry and find the earthly unity and harmony they have looked for. For the brokenhearted who long for a restoration of a marriage, never forget the willingness and power of God to restore relationships when hearts are open and bent to his voice. I know of a mother who prayed for seventeen years—yes, seventeen—until she saw her son and his wife reunited. Nonetheless, it is ever true that we are complete in God, not completed by a man.

The resurrected life of Christ infused into every believer, both woman and man, is the source of sustaining love—a love that is the soil from which harmony, unity, and commitment grows. The morass of misunderstanding in marriage requires forever forgiving one another. In the new creation race, the ability to overcome the strife stirred up because of selfishness is now possible because the old person is dead and we live to serve one another. The wife who knows she is in Christ is able to square her personal freedom, the sanctity of her individuality, and the guarding of her sacred space with the servant heart of the Lord Jesus Christ. She will die to her selfish propensities in order that the marriage may live.

Does the Single Woman Need Male Covering?

SINGLENESS IS ONE of the most underrated human conditions in our culture. Of all people, Christians should realize and embrace the potential for holiness in the single state. Yet many churches shuffle single men and women out of the mainstream of activities into a special group where they can deal with their "singleness" and hopefully connect with someone of the opposite sex!

Married women should support their single sisters and help them see the holiness of their status. Writing to the church at Corinth, Paul wrote in I Corinthians 7:34, "An unmarried woman or virgin is concerned about the Lord's affairs: Her aim is to be devoted to the Lord in both body and spirit."

Author Lauren Winner wrote a review on a new genre of Christian "chick lit" and expressed disappointment that the plots in these novels didn't reflect the potential glory in singleness. "Indeed, for Christians, marriage and singleness are not merely 'lifestyle options,' they are callings, and both the state of marriage and the state of singleness have something to teach the church," she writes. "What marriage teaches the church is something about the communion between people that is now possible through Jesus Christ; what singleness teaches the church is the eschatological reality that singleness, as it were, trumps marriage. Singleness reminds the church that our most basic and fundamental relationship is not that of husband and wife, or parent and child, but with Christ and the rest of the church, as His bride."[9]

So if singleness, as perfectly modeled by Jesus himself, is so desirable and holy, why would single women need to concern themselves with issues of submission, headship, and "male covering" that the Bible addresses to married women?

The answer lies in the fact that they were created female, with all the glories and characteristics of the gender. Since men have been tasked with providing leadership in the church and the home, it is the wise single woman who realizes that while Jesus Christ is her direct head she also needs accountability to a male authority figure in her life—be it a brother, father, friend, or pastor who can provide her with a masculine perspective on life's choices and decisions.

During my seven years as a single mom, I often relied on the verse I found in Isaiah 54:5: "For your Maker is your husband—the LORD Almighty is his name." I take great comfort in knowing that should I ever lose my second earthly husband, once again I will be wedded directly to the Lord. Yet I know I would also seek the advice of godly men before making critical decisions. My two sons would be at the top of that list.

My friend Beth, forty-five, would like to be married but doesn't let her single state keep her from fulfilling her roles as a Christian woman. Active in her church and the favorite aunt of her nieces and nephews, she is a life-giver in so many

NANCY

ways. Beth owns her own home, manages a business that supports her, and gives generously of her time and resources to a multitude of friends and acquaintances.

Still, she says, "I seem to innately know that I need to involve men in my decisions from time to time. I once went to an elder in our church over a financial issue, and I'm blessed to have close friends who are comfortable with my consulting their husbands whenever I need to. As a single woman, I definitely feel the need to seek the wisdom and perspective of men."

The admonition to single women to remember to include men in their lives in significant, authoritative ways in no way diminishes the beauty of the gift that is theirs. Elisabeth Elliot, speaking particularly of the single woman who is a virgin, wrote, "In a way not open to the married woman her daily 'living sacrifice' is a powerful and humble witness, radiating love. I believe she may enter into the 'mystery' more deeply than the rest of us."[10]

ALICE

THIS IS WHERE the headship issue falls on its tail. That the Scriptures do not even use the particular term "male covering" has not caused even a blip on the patriarchal radar screen. Using the term to apply to married women is outrageous enough in the light of the new creation, but to subjugate the unmarried woman with this edict is untenable. Yet its use is familiar to most of us and many may never have investigated either its origin or intent. The Scripture verses from which tradition erroneously extracts this tenet is woven into Paul's first letter to the church at Corinth (1 Cor. 11:3-16).

This gathering of believers was rife with many problems: lawsuits one against the other, divided loyalties to leadership, and even incest. Then to top it off there was this confusing issue of head coverings, which they implored Paul to answer. Before Jewish men became Christians, they were the ones who wore head coverings during worship to show shame for sin, but now, for redeemed men to cover their heads in the presence of God showed that they did not yet fully comprehend the completed work of redemption. Verse 4 reveals this: "Every man who prays or prophesies with his head covered dishonors his head." His head was, of course, Christ. Whether some of the newly ransomed women had already caught on and realized that they were free to uncover their heads—and that this had caused the contention—is not clear. (Some theologians attest to this being one of the most difficult pieces of Scripture to exegete.) We cannot avoid the fact that the Grecian cultural imprint is strong here when we consider that in most ancient societies—and still today in many Middle Eastern countries—women's heads were permanently covered.

What is clear is that although the head and the hair discussions were significant as symbols of spirituality when Paul wrote regarding Christian conduct in AD 56, most of us in the twenty-first century have no such symbolism attached to our rank and spiritual status. Christ is the one and only "covering" required; he is so much more than that—he is an indwelling reality. He intended and accomplished more than any religious ritual could ever symbolize by becoming our very life. Women, we are truly loosed, loved, and liberated.

And cheering us on from the great cloud of witnesses—fully loosed from the shackles of earth—are stellar examples of single women whose legacy should inspire both unmarried and married women alike. Teresa of Avila, the sixteenth-century Spanish contemplative, encourages our empowerment through intimacy with God. Gerald G. May writes of her in *The Dark Night of the Soul*, "In the end, she surrendered—neither to her own judgments nor those of her spiritual directors, but to God alone."[11] Henrietta Mears is known for her colorful hats and her mentoring of both Bill Bright of Campus Crusade for Christ and the renowned evangelist Billy Graham as young men.[12] Today we have the inspiration of our present Secretary of State, Condoleezza Rice, who quipped, "I do think that sometimes there's a misunderstanding that if you did not marry, that you somehow do not have a life. I've read that, you know, about myself from time to time."[13] She is a fine role model of poise and purpose and singleness.

Divorcees and widows increasingly swell the ranks of singles. With more divorces and women living longer than men, congregations may now comprise as high as a quarter of unmarried congregants. The female component of that statistic is a considerable source of unharnessed power. Yet it is often in the church that single women confront the biggest obstacles. In the company of the redeemed, single women are often found in holding patterns until "the real thing comes along." I count many single women in my circle of friends, and the tales of their imposed second-class status are legendary. One particular woman who was very gifted both in music and teaching was given only limited opportunity to do both, mainly where she would not be seen as—Lord forbid—directing the choir in full view on Sunday morning. The repeated injunction from the leadership was, "Once you are married and covered by your husband we will feel free to let you teach and play publicly." Does that imply that in her private life she is uncovered? What kind of covering protects her when she prays by her bedside every night; when she rescues one of her students at school from suicide? For the benefit of whom do leaders impose this charade? It is illogical.

The lack of logic did not escape the notice of our Jesus when he commissioned women to be the first to broadcast the news of the resurrection. Lack of "covering" did not constrain him in his selection of a single woman by the name of Mary of Magdala to be the first to hear these world-changing words, "Go instead to my brothers and tell them, 'I am returning to my Father and your Father, to my God and your God'" (John 20:17).

All the redeemed—female and male, children, widowed, divorced, or single—comprise the bride of Christ. We are the betrothed, and the consummation of the promise awaits all believers. Single women are not wives-in-waiting but a chosen part of the body of Christ awaiting the marriage supper of the Lamb. Being married can never solicit more of God's love than he already lavishes on the single woman. It is time to take the stigma—the *sin*—out of single and embrace one another as entire, whole, wanting nothing and no one: the only "covering" is that of love that covers a multitude of sins.

— ALICE

CAN A LESBIAN BE A CHRISTIAN?

ONE NIGHT IN May years ago I walked the streets of Manhattan with a male friend and coworker who confessed to me that ever since he was a little boy he'd felt more at home in the kitchen with the women after Thanksgiving dinner than in the den with the men watching football. The night before he'd taken a gay lover. My husband and I sat in a Chinese restaurant across the table from dear Christian friends another night, listening as they poured out the news that their daughter was entering into a lesbian relationship. We all cried. My favorite housepainter is a lesbian living with a partner and her children. She's my favorite because she's a reliable, hard worker and just plain fun to be around.

I say all this not to establish the "I'm cool because I have gay friends" credential some of my liberal acquaintances seem to wear like a badge, but to establish that although I'm a conservative

— NANCY

Christian I'm not an "ivory tower" one, and I'm certainly not homophobic.

Can a lesbian be a Christian? Absolutely if she has accepted Jesus Christ as her Savior and Lord. What so many in the church fail to recognize is that although homosexuality is a sin, it's no worse than any other sin in the eyes of God. All sin is equally deplored by him and makes him weep. A lesbian can be a Christian in the same way an alcoholic, a person who commits adultery, or someone who cheats on income tax can be a Christian. The sanctification process, which leads us to be more like Jesus every day, begins the moment we accept him and are indwelled by the Holy Spirit. Yet most of us tentatively hold on to certain areas of our lives that we aren't quite ready to surrender. For the Christian lesbian, it's her sexuality.

Obviously homosexuality is a blatant abuse of manhood and womanhood as God designed them. Leviticus 18:22 declares it "detestable" and in Romans 1:27 Paul calls homosexual acts a "perversion." How is a Christian woman to embrace this truth and still love her lesbian neighbor as herself?

The answer lies in the simple practice possible only through the power of Jesus Christ to do as he would do: hate the sin, but love the sinner. Again and again throughout the Gospels we see Jesus responding to sinners this way as he spoke the truth in love, and we are to do the same. It's only when we are able to love them that we may be able to gently expose them to biblical truth. If they are already believers, the Holy Spirit may convict them to leave their lives of sin. If they are not believers, they may be led to become so by our loving relationship with them, not by our condemnation. Once they believe, we can trust the Holy Spirit to do his work.

Those without a Christian worldview can't understand the "hate the sin, but love the sinner" concept. They can't understand that through the power of the Holy Spirit it's possible for Christians to accept their homosexual friends and neighbors, loving them exactly as they are, without approving of their lifestyle choices. And so Christian organizations like Focus on the Family, taking a stand for Christian marriage and traditional family values and trying to educate the public as to the very detrimental effects of the homosexual agenda in education and politics, are labeled "hate mongers" and "homophobic." Nothing could be further from the truth.

I'm aware that I called homosexuality a lifestyle choice in the last paragraph. Although some report of a "gay gene"—and it is possible—those studies are high on media attention and low on conclusive data. Obviously the push is there to establish this link because homosexuality can then be fully mainstreamed as a natural condition, not a perversion. Homosexuals could feel justified knowing they had no other choice; it was just "in the cards." I honestly don't know if homosexuality is the result of a lifestyle choice, a defect in what was once a perfect human design, or both. I only know that regardless of the cause, by the grace of God it is redeemable.

Where Grace Abounds, a wonderful organization in Denver, Colorado, provides emotional support and healing for gays and those who love them. They commit to 100 percent grace and 100 percent truth, with no compromise, and take the approach that inappropriate sexual behavior of all kinds is a symptom of a reparative drive which is attempting to resolve much deeper issues such as spiritual emptiness, unresolved emotional trauma, and unmet intimacy and love needs. That it is, in effect, a counterfeit solution for a genuine problem.[14]

One of my concerns is that homosexuality is also becoming "cool." Whereas the teenage girl disappointed or ignored by boys in the past might have channeled her frustration into mastering a sport or forging a career, she's much more likely now to say, "To heck with boys, I'll just be a lesbian and get all the attention and companionship I need." Unfortunately, a good part of our culture would applaud her choice.

Today's Christian woman interested in modeling and supporting biblical womanhood must be aware of the power of the activist homosexual agenda in America today—and ready with love and biblical truth for her friends, her daughters, and her lesbian sisters. She needs to understand that the success of the gay marriage agenda threatens biblical marriage and families, and is not just a "live and let live" issue. Especially when children are involved.

For the protection of our families and culture, our prayer for our lesbian sister needs to be that

NANCY

she will draw on the power of God to come out of her sinful lifestyle. If she isn't able to enter into a healthy heterosexual relationship, may she employ the same self-denial relied upon by Christians who are addicts, by virtuous single women, by widows, and by others who get the power to abstain from the One who sustains us all. If she doesn't, we are still called to love her because Jesus died for us all.

ALICE

TEARS WELLED UP in her luminous blue eyes. As she lifted her hand to wipe away the tears that trickled down her cheek, I saw the massive tattoo that spread out over her arm and shoulder—an eagle in flight. This woman is well acquainted with flight; she is familiar with having to flee disapproval and having to hide from rejection. Now she is equally acquainted with what the eagle depicts; the ability to soar in full view, like a bird in the skies of God's limitless love. My friend is a Christian and a lesbian.

For many in the church, the coupling of the words *lesbian* and *Christian* is an oxymoron. If that is true, then linking an assortment of other words with the term *Christian* should be equally anathema. Gluttons who claim they are part of the body of Christ; jealous women who say they are believers; women who have committed adultery yet stand firm in their position as a follower of Jesus. Even if some in the church concede that a woman in a homosexual lifestyle can be born again, they seem to find it far easier to accept the overeater.

As much as we tout a gospel of grace, the strong root of the law has worked its tentacles so deep into our subconscious that we are unaware of the legalism we spout and spread to those whose actions we either don't understand or of whom we disapprove. (I have noticed that our lack of understanding does not usually deter us from ratcheting up the disapproval quotient.) The quick riposte at this point is usually something like, "But homosexuality is expressly forbidden in the Bible." Then we walk away feeling vindicated, careless of the pain and hurt we have inflicted and ignorant of our own sinful hubris.

We are all well versed in the Scriptures that challenge homosexuality. The "detestable" verse from Leviticus 18:22 is usually the one in "second coming" size print that Christians carry at gay pride marches. From chapter 1 of Paul's letter to the Roman church we have explicit reference to same sex activity that is part of a list of offenses, which includes envy, strife, greed, malice, heartlessness, ruthlessness, and disobedience to parents (Rom. 1:29–31). The apostle wraps it up by saying, "You therefore, have no excuse, you who pass judgment on someone else, for at whatever point you judge the other, you are condemning yourself, because you who pass judgment do the same things" (Rom. 2:1).

If we read these first few chapters in Romans—where the writer is establishing the case for humankind's inability to have a relationship with God without heaven's intervention—we finally find the solution in the first two verses of chapter 5. "Therefore, since we have been justified through faith, we have peace with God through our Lord Jesus Christ, through whom we have gained access by faith into this grace in which we now stand." The atoning work that bought our peace was not death for a host of sins—rated according to their gravity where homosexuality repeatedly ranks high—but a death that took care of the sin nature, the source of all sins (Rom. 6:6). He replaced that nature with his very own life—our unrighteousness for his righteousness.

We walk, live, and love in this great abounding grace of God. By this grace, he has birthed us into his family and we cry "Abba Father" together. "There is no asterisk over my name that excludes me from the family of God" as another lesbian sister said. Let us leave the final judging to the Father—it is his job to discipline and train the children whom he has birthed into his family, not the siblings." As Rowland Croucher, in an article titled "Homosexuality: An Interview with Jesus" writes, "Law is to love what railway tracks are to the train: the law gives direction, but all the propulsive power is in the train."[15]

Then let us lavishly cherish, respect, and love one another. The Greek words that differentiate kinds of love are lost when, in English, the word *love* is used singularly to describe anything and everything that we like. *Agapē* describes the unconditional God kind of love. I like to use the analogy of a beam of sunlight that hits the earth and sheds its light on the garbage dump and the rose garden alike. It does not discriminate for it just *is*. God *is* love—it is not just something he does. The other Greek words *ēros, philiō,* and *storgē* describe the gamut of human love—all operate with conditions of acceptance. Without accessing the *agapē* love that is in us, our best effort at loving is only human love to the nth degree and ends up woefully conditional. Our limited human love is incapable of loving the unlovely and unlovable—tragically, the categories into which lesbians are usually assigned. God's love and ours, by his gifting and grace, is a steady beam of acceptance, approval, and compassion on all.

The hallmark of this grace and love is in the outstretched hand, the loving embrace of one humble, worshipful, and grateful prodigal to another. It is not assembling to march, to protest, and to denigrate another human being in whom the Spirit of God lives. We are nothing without unconditional love—what part of nothing is it that we do not understand?

Reconciling Our Differences

Although we passionately hold disparate views on feminism, we still let love rule. We leave the outcome of choices to the Father—those of divorce and homosexuality included. We both have tasted of his mercy and know we can trust him with solutions to these challenging issues.

Chapter 7

Leaving Our Hearts Behind
A Lasting Legacy

*There are only two lasting bequests we
can hope to give our children.
One of these is roots: the other wings.*

—HODDING CARTER

HOW CAN WE DISTINGUISH FREEDOM FROM OPPRESSION?

ALICE

SIX MONTHS IN quarantine can't be fun. But if our beloved springer spaniel, Rabbie, was to come with us when we returned to live in England that's exactly what he would have to do. And he was to come with us. We faithfully visited him every week and then painfully took our leave of him as the door of the kennel closed behind us. Then the eagerly anticipated day of his homecoming arrived. This time the gate was wide open as we stood waiting for our exuberant four-legged friend to bound out: but Rabbie did not move. He did not know he was free—so accustomed had he become to the confines of his kennel. This is a vivid illustration of being unable to distinguish freedom from imprisonment or oppression.

We can become so accustomed to invisible walls and fences of restriction that we are unable to see doors of choice wide open and freedom beckoning. In a toxic relationship—or one dominated by the doctrine of male supremacy, for example—we are not even aware that we are in a prison of confinement, restriction, and oppression until we experience the epiphany that our life energy is seeping out of us, that we no longer know who we are—that we are hemorrhaging from our heart. Then, by God's grace, we glimpse a silhouette of hope on the horizon—a hope that we can live another way. The next step, be it a baby one or a giant stride, is the one that transforms the shadow of hope into substance as we courageously embark on a journey towards the full, free, and fearless life that our Savior has bought for us.

How do we distinguish freedom from oppression? Whether in marriage or friendship, in the workplace or in our religious lives, the litmus test is the presence of fear. Respect and consideration of another's needs or values is very different from fearing the consequences of voicing our own opinions or acting on the strength of our own convictions. If fear is the inhibitor of our tentative moves and tiny steps in the dance of intimacy, or if we tremble at the prospect of what a false step might incur—disdain, dismissal, or abuse—then we know we are not free to be ourselves, to make mistakes, or to think independently. We are controlled, captivated, and kept prisoner—not by another—but by our own fear. We are often oblivious of our complicity in our capture until the grace of God lifts the veil of deception.

The veil that indicates a woman's inferior status to men is highly visible in the world where they wear the burkah. In a world without burkahs, women in the Western world who embrace the complementarian stance have chosen to wear a less visible, but nonetheless real garment of subjugation to men. I wonder how excited our Muslim sister would be if we told her that, on becoming a Christian, she could discard the outward evidence of inferiority but would still have to remain in a secondary position to men.

For a female to be beholden to another human being is anathema to the freedom we have been given in Christ. When we can see clearly—free of the real and the virtual tokens of our oppression—then we are empowered to take responsibility for our own life. And, for our disobedience to him. Yes, disobedience to God—for at some level we have surrendered to fear rather than to love, and in so doing have given another the lordship in our lives that belongs to God alone.

That lordship is his right. We are not our own, for the Father has bought us with a high price (1 Cor. 6:19–20). We may grope and grovel for a long time in the wilderness of our own willfulness but, true to his promise to work everything

ALICE

for our good, he hounds us until we come home—this is the inescapable love of God. "The Israelites of the Old Testament were lucky," writes Sarah Ban Breathnach in her probing book *Something More*. "They wandered in the Wilderness for only forty years. Most of us stumble through the trial, terror, and triumphs of life's terrain a lot longer, usually until we're ready, willing, and able to come face-to-face with the truth about ourselves: what magnificent, extraordinary, glorious, powerful, courageous, and lovable beings we are.... But we don't know we're worthy of *being* loved until we set out in search of the Promised Land or stumble toward Something More."[1]

Our something more is a some*one* more. Our gracious God has prepared a Promised Land where he meets our every need in the person of the Lord Jesus Christ. He is the door to our freedom. He is the liberator from our oppression. Let the ache, the longing, and the loneliness of our hearts propel us to that place—to that person who is now within us—a place where no bars, no shackles, no padlocks can incarcerate us.

NANCY

THE FIRST WOMEN ever to vote in Iraq proudly held up the fingers they had dipped in purple ink at the polls for all the world to see. When we think of oppressed women we think of those who have yet to vote. Those who walk streets in the Middle East in complete burkahs without even their eyes exposed. We think of women in Africa wondering where to find food for their starving children. But we need to broaden our definition of what it means to be an oppressed woman.

In our own culture, the oppressed woman is the executive who finds out she'll be out of town for her son's birthday ... again. She's the woman who gets up each morning thinking she has to do everything at home and at work or it simply won't get done right. She's the young married woman who sees marriage as a power struggle and is constantly assessing who's winning.

All of these women, along with those suffering under political and physical oppression, find it difficult to find freedom in the midst of their circumstances. In fact, the harder they work at grasping it, the more elusive it becomes. The Christian woman needs to remember that it is in Christ, and him only, that true freedom is hers to claim. In John 8:32 Jesus said, "Then you will know the truth, and the truth will set you free." The reason so many women in our society today don't feel free is because a great deal of biblical truth has been obscured by the feminist agenda and by the values and mores of our culture. A woman today is "free to choose." Free to choose what? Free to choose to end the life of her unborn baby. Certainly not the kind of freedom Jesus encouraged believers to embrace.

In her Bible study *Becoming a Woman of Freedom*, Cynthia Heald writes, "When I am discouraged, I begin to pray. I tell the Lord my feelings and ask him to help me understand why I'm depressed. The reasons vary—sin, tiredness,

NANCY

believing the enemy, not trusting God. I find that if I seek the truth about my circumstances, then it is the truth that can set me free to trust Him and to receive His grace and guidance in the midst of my adversity."[2]

The truth of God's Word, especially the gospel message of salvation through Jesus, is the truth that sets us free. Extreme positions of feminism or legalism in the church may try to rob us of the freedom that grace guarantees. But through an understanding of the tenets of biblical womanhood found in the whole counsel of God's Word, women can come out of the darkness of confusion, sin, and self-doubt and into the sunshine of freedom. Through faith in Jesus Christ, we are even free from death, for "if the Son sets you free, you will be free indeed" (John 8:36).

HOW CAN OLDER WOMEN BEST MENTOR YOUNGER ONES?

ALICE

I HAVE LONG pondered why so few older women mentor younger women and have concluded that the reason is twofold. First, in an age where aging is anathema to beauty and productivity—where the culture of youth rules—we are loathe to admit that we are "the older." Second, in an era generally characterized by a "go it alone" mentality, the younger women often exhibit no need to solicit the wisdom of the ancients who, unlike their Eastern counterparts, are not held in great honor and respect. (Chinese custom consoles the young with the prospect of being old and finally being held in high regard.)

The young certainly should give more honor to their elders; however, the elders have to recognize that wisdom is not the prerogative of the aged (Job 32:6-10), but rather the fruit of the Spirit that is in a person. Job's fourth and youngest counselor, Elihu, after hearing the endless harangues of his elders as they berated their bewildered companion Job, observed that their words were far from being wise. Therefore, for the older woman, the first consideration for mentoring eligibility is, "Will I speak from the wisdom of the Spirit of Christ that is in me or deliver dogma, personal prejudice, and unlived principles?"

Without doubt, words are cheap. It appears that some of us have kissed the proverbial Blarney Stone before we could walk, so full of verbiage are we! However, what speaks loudest is what we *do*. Do we walk in dependence on our God? Do we live authentically, willing to be vulnerable to expose our own weaknesses and failures? If we bill our act as, "Come hear me, I have all the answers"; if we present ourselves as self-righteous; if we claim to have fail-safe formulas for a zinging marriage or for producing trouble-free offspring—we do our hearers and ourselves a grave disservice.

We are representations of Christ, and our goal in mentoring is to live a life that reflects the irresistible beauty of Jesus, a life lived in utter dependence on the Father, a life that points others to him, not to us. The greatest gift we can give to anyone is the assurance of being totally accepted in the Beloved and that God will complete the work he has begun in all of us. The greatest obstacle we can put in anyone's way is to fetter them with formulaic living—principles, yes—but rigid "one size fits all" garments suffocate and constrict their unique expression of Christ.

Previous chapters are replete with illustrations of the choices that women have to make in order to fulfill their own destiny—single or married, childless or not, in the pulpit or in the pew. Our most effective mentoring is primarily modeling the results of choices freely made in our own lives. The more we are at home in our own skins—the more confident of our own individuality and destiny—the more effective will be our influence on younger women.

My mother passed that confidence on to me—though it felt like abandonment at the time—when a mere week after my first little one was born she returned to her home with these parting words. "You will find your own way of organizing and operating, and it will be the best way for both you and your baby." That little girl, now fully adult, confirmed this truth with me recently. "I'm grateful for what you taught me, Mom, but now it comes down to my own theology—what I believe and know about my God that will see me through." Another younger woman recently told me, after years of being in my Bible studies, "The greatest gift you have given me is how to think for myself." That thrills my heart.

If we do not encourage another to think freely, the danger of spiritual abuse ever lurks in the shadows. In the church this is not only possible, but tragically, quite prevalent. The stronger taking the weaker under one's wing—while necessary at times—can become the breeding ground for subtle and sometimes overt abuse of both the person we are mentoring and the privilege of being a mentor. In the general religious arena, we are probably more familiar with the sexual abuse that people—particularly women and children—often suffer at the hands of a trusted person in authority. In the realm of women mentoring other women, the greatest potential for abuse happens when the weaker or younger starts to gain strength and confidence. It is then that we who are mature must be ready to let them fly, to flee our own need to be needed, and not inflict either our paradigm or pathology onto them.

The best mentoring then is the kind that exalts the Lord Jesus as sufficient and that exhorts our younger sibling in the Lord never to accept any substitute guide for direction—to know his voice above all others. "Greatly should we rejoice that God dwells in our soul," writes the renowned fourteenth-century mystic Julian of Norwich, one who was intimate and well acquainted with the voice of her God, "—and rejoice yet more because our soul dwells in God. Our soul is created to be God's home and the soul is at home in the uncreated God."[3]

IT WAS A bit of a shock to me when women in my church began seeking my counsel. They wanted the wisdom and opinions of "an older woman," but that inner part of me that says "I'm just a girl at heart" wanted to run away and hide—not listen with an ear to counseling and directing. But soon I began to realize that by virtue of my years, my life experiences, and my walk with the Lord through good times and bad, I did have some wisdom to share. Not lessons developed on yellow legal pads in the wee hours of the morning, but lessons the Lord engraved on my heart.

More than any other lesson learned, it is the truth the Lord showed me about biblical womanhood, the truth I'm writing about in this book, that fills my heart with passion—and the feeling that I want to run out and stop women on the street to share the good news with them! After all, had I been exposed earlier to this truth, my heart would bear fewer scars.

Yet I've learned that not only can God use our painful experiences, he specializes in using them. "Praise be to the God and Father of our Lord Jesus Christ, the Father of compassion and the God of all comfort, who comforts us in all our troubles, so that we can comfort those in any trouble with the comfort we ourselves have received from God" (2 Cor. 1:3–4).

When we walk through various trials and sufferings and emerge on the other side "persecuted, but not abandoned; struck down, but not destroyed" (2 Cor. 4:9), God uses those experiences to create a bridge from our heart to someone else's. Their value is apparent in this story. My husband once decided he wanted to lead a Bible study at a detention center for juvenile offenders near his office building. Excitedly he prepared his lessons and week after week he faithfully showed up for the study, but he could tell the Spirit wasn't at work there. "I'm not supposed to be the one leading those boys to Christ," he realized after some disappointment and prayer. "They need to hear the truth from someone who's been down the same path they're on now."

As women we all have something to share about the paths we've been down, and it's in the sharing that hearts are opened. I volunteer for one-to-one Bible study with young single moms who live in a residential facility with their children not far from my house. When I first meet the woman I'm assigned to mentor, I can tell by the look on her face that she's thinking, "What could this 'church chat' lady possibly know about my struggles." But as soon as I share that I've been divorced and was a single mother for seven years, the expression on her face totally changes. Suddenly she's open to hearing what I want to share about grace and forgiveness. That's God using my mistakes for his glory!

So how do older women, whether older in years or in spiritual maturity, best mentor younger ones? Simply by being willing to share what they have learned from the Lord in a spirit of truth and love. By faithfully committing the time to listen, by relying on the Holy Spirit to tell them what to say when and when to let a silent hug or tear say it all.

Teaching ability or experience isn't a requirement for mentoring; being willing to use your own life as an example is. You also don't have to have all the answers. The wise mentor is one who knows when to say, "I don't know, but let's take this problem to the Lord together and trust him with it." She knows that a mentoring relationship that includes being in the Word and regularly praying with one another is one with fewer opportunities for failure. It's also one guaranteed to bring as much growth and joy to the mentor as to the woman she mentors.

Mentoring can be as informal as a conversation over the back fence or as organized as a mentoring program in the women's ministry at a church, but however the two women come together, you can be sure it will be the Lord who brings them heart to heart. A pastor writing about a woman in his church who mentored many young women said, "Her ministry does not have the feel of formality; it has the feel of family. The Lord leads her one step at a time to women with whom to spend time."[4]

If you are an older woman willing to enter into a mentoring relationship, spend time around younger women. Invite them over for a much-needed, restorative afternoon tea, or volunteer to go shopping with them to help them keep the kids in tow. If you have a special skill you can pass on to another generation—be it quilting, accounting, or interior design—offer to give classes or private instruction. God can use all those relationships to open the door to a life-changing mentoring experience.

"Spiritual mothering relationships come in all shapes and sizes," Susan Hunt writes. "There is no formula. This ministry is not a program, it is a lifestyle."[5] Additionally, she says, "Titus 2 relationships are never random. They are always life-giving. The purpose is God's glory, and the authority is God's Word."[6]

If you dropped my Bible it might automatically fall open at Titus 2:3–5, for I go there often for inspiration and the encouraging reminder that because of Jesus—not because of the life I've lived or the holiness of my own soul apart from him—I am worthy to be the "older woman" in a mentoring relationship. "Likewise, teach the older women to be reverent in the way they live, not to be slanderers or addicted to much wine, but to teach what is good," the passage begins. Many of the young women I see where I volunteer suffer from some sort of addiction. They may be fighting an addiction to drugs or alcohol, or to the equally destructive need to be wanted by a man—just any man. I need to be free of addiction in order to lead them in Bible study. Then, if it's God's will, each one will be able to replace self-indulgence with self-control, a fruit of the Spirit. Opening the Bible is also the best way to teach what is good—for it's the story of God's relationship with his people and God is good, all the time.

"Then they can train the younger women to love their husbands and children, to be self-controlled and pure ..." the passage continues. It's the selflessness of love that needs to be taught and modeled here. If God has blessed us with husbands and children, we are to love them no matter what. Again, it's only through the power of the Holy Spirit that we can learn to love unconditionally as we have been loved. Being self-controlled and pure in our daily lives, by his grace, is how we love ourselves.

"To be busy at home, to be kind, and to be subject to their husbands, so that no one will malign the word of God," the passage concludes. You may find it odd that Paul would include submission in a sentence with being productive at home and being kind, but since submission is primarily a picture of humility it fits perfectly. There's joy in keeping a functional, pleasant home for your husband and children. Kindness is its own reward as we carry God's love into the world through our selfless interactions with others. Submission secures the success of the marriage that holds the home and family together. And all these things bring glory to God's Word—and to him.

"Paul was smart enough to know that women need women to train them how to apply God's Word to areas of our lives that are uniquely feminine," Susan Hunt writes in *Spiritual Mothering*. "In this command, older women are given the high calling of traditioning biblical womanhood. This is not a ministry of minutia; it is a vital part of church life that must not be pushed to the backburner."[7]

NANCY

Cover yourself with prayer and ask others to pray for you. Be willing to open up your life, with all its ugliness and all its beauty, as an example to women who are on the path behind you. God will honor your efforts as you live for him and simply allow another woman to watch and learn.

What Will We Leave Our Daughters and Granddaughters?

ALICE

A NINETY-SIX-YEAR-OLD organist played the offertory music at church this past Mother's Day. As her granddaughter led the frail but focused old woman up to the platform, I wondered what kind of legacy this particular woman was leaving to her family. I am sure that her granddaughter felt proud and privileged to be that noble lady's escort. When the grandmother introduced the pieces that she would play, she was not content to simply play a traditional rendition of "Amazing Grace," but added, "I am going to do a jazzed-up version as well." She had lost neither her love and touch for music nor her passion and love for life.

A very special connection exists between children and their grandparents. The love we have for our granddaughters is one that—although no greater than that which we have for our daughters—has been distilled over the years into a purer essence of expression. It is relatively free from the sediments of anxiety, frustration, and fear that pollute the mother's perspective. I recall with great pride and gratitude my own grandmothers. I remember my paternal grandmother peering closely at the weekly newspaper then, with her pale blue eyes flashing, spouting her own vociferous opinions on the Island's news. Those same sparkling eyes would be warm and tear-filled as she squeezed some pennies into my hand for "sweeties" when I left for home.

The memory of my maternal grandmother is of a woman of settled security in her Savior and established in serenity despite ravaging losses. She is the one who imparted the revelation about loving yourself before you can love others that I recounted in the prologue. In recollecting what they each left me, their images take on shape and form and, after all those years, my senses still fill up with their smells, sounds, and touch.

We will all leave a legacy of some kind—that is unavoidable. Each life has painful past places of remorse and regret, but these mistakes need not detract from the legacy we leave our progeny. In fact, the more they can see of the grace of God in our lives, the greater his appeal to be able to help them in their weaknesses. This kind of vulnerability is a very powerful place from which to encourage our daughters as they struggle with their own inadequacies, fears, and failures—whether through shipwrecked marriages or prodigal children. "Though the soul's wounds heal, the scars remain," writes Julian of Norwich. "God sees them not as blemishes but as honours."[8]

Jesus' scars will remain for all eternity—a lasting testament of his passion, purpose, and love. Such an archetype is an appropriate model by which to measure our own legacy. In this book, for example, both Nancy and I set out to state our convictions with passion—staying true to our purpose—without sacrificing our love for one another. My passion is that women know who they are in Christ and learn to walk in that limitless love and freedom in every area of their lives. The torch of freedom that God has entrusted to me, I carry to others. I can do no less.

Whatever passion or purpose propels us, the legacy of love is the deposit from which our children and their children will make withdrawals down through the generations. If we do not have the benefit of a loving natural family, we need not despair. God delights in redressing the balances and giving us a bounty of riches from which we can freely bequeath a passion and a purpose out of the new, supernatural life he has given to us in Christ Jesus.

One such woman who learned how to overcome a lack of love and still leave an impressive legacy was Abigail Scott Duniway. When she drew her first breath in a little log cabin in Tazewell County, Illinois, on October 22, 1834, her mother wept and her father was angry that she was not a boy. She started her life as a burden, yet, "With less than a sixth-grade education, Abigail Duniway became a noted journalist and prominent suffragist who gained recognition as a dedicated leader for women's rights. She endured hardship, deprivation, ridicule, and sneers as she fought a forty-two-year battle to achieve her goal, becoming the first woman in Oregon to register to vote in a national election."9

Remaining true to ourselves in a world filled with murky motives, half-truths, and a staggering lack of integrity results in a rare and precious commodity for our children to lay claim to in our name. Coupling our passion with love is a rock-solid investment that will resist the vagaries of the market—the changing mores, the fluctuating standards, and the whims of the world system.

When my maternal grandmother said goodbye to this world, her assurance in the Lord at the moment of death was as sure as her confidence in him throughout her long life. As her daughters stood by the bedside their mother took flight for heaven singing, "Jesus, Lover of my soul/Let me to Thy bosom fly."10 So she sealed her legacy for all time. What she lived and left lives on in me—and in my daughter and granddaughter.

NANCY

BEFORE MY TEENAGE granddaughter becomes a day older I'm hoping for the development of some procedure that would allow me to transfer everything I learned the hard way painlessly into her heart and mind. Maybe then she would realize the rich tradition of biblical womanhood that is hers. Maybe then she would be able to maintain the purity and focus God desires for her benefit. Maybe then.

Yet even as I write this I realize the Creator already put a plan in place for transferring this information. It's the charge he gives mothers and grandmothers to pass along life's lessons and hold their children and grandchildren up in prayer daily. "I have been reminded of your sincere faith, which first lived in your grandmother Lois and in your mother Eunice and, I am persuaded, now lives in you also" (2 Tim. 1:5), Paul wrote to Timothy. The influence we have on future generations is undeniable, and we must not let our fear of being rejected as "uncool" keep us from sharing the truth we have.

In her book *What Our Mothers Didn't Tell Us*, Danielle Crittenden writes from the heart of a woman who wishes she had inherited such truth. Though writing from a secular viewpoint, she concludes that happiness often eludes the modern woman because her mother, the feminist, passed along lies rather than truth regarding a woman's truest purpose. In one particularly heartrending passage she says, "We want the warm body next to us on the sofa in the evenings; we want the noise and embrace of a family around us; we want, at the end of our lives, to look back and see that what we have done amounts to more than a pile of pay stubs, that we have loved and been loved, and brought into this world life that will outlast us."[11]

What do I want to pass on to my stepdaughters, daughters-in-law, and granddaughters? All the truth about biblical womanhood I've shared in this book: the importance of purity, an understanding of the beauty and power of a marriage that honors God, the rich tradition they have as women, and an appreciation for the inherent, created beauty that is their incomparable gift from God. They are beautiful in his eyes, and the world's standards mean nothing.

I want them to believe that they can do anything and everything to which they devote their lives, but encourage them to choose carefully in order to bring God the glory. Somehow I want to save them from the ravages of a culture that would drag them down into valleys of despair rather than lift them up to the heights, for the view of life is so much better up high! Yet I know that it's not I, but God, who can accomplish all these things.

Purity is such an old-fashioned sounding word, but just think what our society would be like if women were pure. The consequences of impurity—venereal disease, abortion, out-of-wedlock babies, and the rampant loss of self-esteem and self-worth—wouldn't exist. Women would enter into marriage whole, without having given away little bits of their souls with each act of illicit sex. They would be free to enjoy their marriage bed and keep it pure (Heb. 13:4) without comparing their husbands' lovemaking with past or extra-marital lovers.

Barbara Mouser writes poignantly about the power and holiness of purity. "The virginity of a nation's women, their purity, is one of the greatest natural and human resources that we have, because virginity is a gateway to two things of monumental importance. First, it is the gateway to a woman's capacity to love a man, and second, to a woman's capacity to give life to children. This gateway should never be opened except in marriage, because when virginity is unlocked, all of a woman's loving response should be allowed to come forth inside a stable relationship.... Children deserve to come forth into a family built on the covenanted love of a man and a woman who will be father and mother to them."[12]

We need to teach our daughters and granddaughters that their purity is a sacred trust. Song of Songs 4:12 says, "You are a garden locked up, my sister, my bride; you are a spring enclosed, a sealed fountain." Even the youngest girls can understand that as women they have a "secret garden" inside them, an inner domain that is theirs to protect until they choose to open it up as a gift for their husbands in marriage.

Purity in women also motivates men to live honorable lives. Barbara Mouser uses the analogy of the princess who, through her alluring purity, motivated the barbarian to save her, and he became king! When good girls go bad, she says, we release the barbarian nature of men into our culture.

In the article "Why God Says Wait," Amy Stephens points out that "Despite what feminists have been telling us for years—that sexual freedom empowers women—according to the report 'The State of Our Unions—Why Men Won't Commit' by the National Marriage Project, the big losers in the sexual freedom movement have been women. When men can get sex for free, why commit to a woman? Men can enjoy the benefits of having a pseudo wife by cohabiting rather than marrying."[13]

We need a "purity revival" in this country, and it needs to begin with mothers and grandmothers passing along truth to counter the messages conveyed by the music lyrics and fashion trends of the culture. For some of us, it also means taking the courageous step of saying, "Don't do what I did, and here's why." The world tells our daughters and granddaughters that it's crazy to deny themselves pleasure by abstaining from sex until marriage. We need to tell them that if they do abstain, God will give them pleasures that those of us who didn't wait will never know.

We must also pass along everything we've learned about marriage, including the fact that men who feel respected by their wives make much better husbands. Dr. Laura Schlessinger has been filling the airwaves with no-nonsense advice about marriage for years, and she summarized many tidbits in her book, *The Proper Care and Feeding of Husbands*. Encouraging women to do less nagging and more loving, she promotes complimenting your husband, appreciating him, and as much as possible, being responsive when he desires to make love. While the feminists cried foul, millions of listeners and readers sent their thanks to Dr. Laura because they took her advice, and their marriages reaped the benefits.

When the wife submits to her husband and the husband loves his wife as Christ loves the church, both halves of the marriage equation are in place and the result is an awesome marriage.

Married men and women are not independent or codependent, but interdependent. That's God's plan for marriage, and we must teach it and model it at every opportunity.

Young married couples often hear the wise biblical advice never to go to bed angry (Eph. 4:26). That is good advice, but they may also need to know how to do that. What keeps me from letting anger take control is simply asking myself how Jesus would respond to the situation, then giving it to him in prayer. By taking things my husband can't change or can't fix to my Lord instead, everything falls into perspective and my anger subsides. I wish all wives could embrace this truth.

Many believe that the complementarian legacy is one of limited options, but that's simply not true. I pray the young women who come after me will have many opportunities to use all their God-given talents, but I also pray they will have the wisdom to make the right choices in each season of life. If they choose to be part of the professional world at some point, I want them to know they can do so without apologizing for, or sacrificing, their femininity, homes, or families.

A female judge reflecting on years of career experience rendered this seasoned opinion: "Perhaps we have come far enough in our progression toward personal and professional equality to recognize and honor those traits that historically represented the feminine in society. We need those traits as people, to be whole. Our chosen professions need those traits as we struggle with increasingly complex problems and systems. Our world needs those traits as we seek to mend deep rifts and reach common solutions."[14]

The jobs those women who follow us take will vary greatly, and may even fall into traditional male arenas. Mentioned throughout the Bible are women whom God asked to temporarily "stand in the gap" and either perform a task ordinarily done by a man or move a man forward to action. So we see the wise and beautiful Abigail petitioning David not to destroy her people in retaliation against her foolish husband Nabal in 1 Samuel 25:24–31. We see Deborah serving as a judge in Israel, holding court under a palm tree, and agreeing to accompany the cowardly Barak to be his talisman in battle in Judges 4–5. And we see Queen Esther biding her time and praying until she had the perfect opportunity to approach King Xerxes and ask that he spare the Jewish people. As Mordecai advised Esther, "who knows but that you have come to royal position for such a time as this?" (Esth. 4:14). When God needs a woman to further his purposes he will give her the task, but he may ask her to stand in without asking her to take over. Our role is to listen carefully and respond appropriately.

When I finished my yearlong study of biblical womanhood I was asked to write a summary of all that the Lord had revealed to me. I chose to do that in the form of a letter addressed to my stepdaughters, daughters-in-law, and the two small granddaughters we had then. In the letter, I shared many of the truths shared with you in this book.

NANCY

"How I wish I could just transfer all God has shown me into your minds and hearts and spare you any of the pain I've gone through," I wrote. "I know that is impossible, however, so I trust that each of you is exactly where God would have you be in your journey as women right now, and that, in his time, he will reveal to you the truths he wants you to see." I closed the letter by saying, "Always rest secure in the knowledge that you are a wonderful, awesome, excellent woman, created by God to be the crown of his creation. Wow!"

It's been almost ten years since I delivered that letter. The legacy of biblical womanhood still offers so much to the women in our family—and to you. The only question is whether you will see the truth or allow the veils of deceit the world puts in place to obscure it from view.

When I think of the wisdom and faith of my grandmothers and my mother I wish I had grasped the legacy they passed on to me sooner. I can only rejoice that I have it now, and my ongoing prayer is Psalm 71:18: "Even when I am old and gray, do not forsake me, O God, till I declare your power to the next generation, your might to all who are to come."

I know I can't spare my teenage granddaughter all the pain and consequences of her choices. As wise and wonderful as she is, she may make some mistakes along the way. I can only pray for her and trust that the Lord has her in his hands. What I can be sure of, however, is that no matter what happens I will always love her. And love is the most lasting legacy of all.

Reconciling Our Differences

Because we view the roles of the Christian woman so differently and have made our choices accordingly, the legacies we leave will be decidedly different. However, we are consistent here as elsewhere in our commitment to leave the greatest legacy of all—love.

Chapter 8

Loving One Another Anyway

Unity in Christ

In essentials, unity, in nonessentials, liberty, and in all things, love.

—S<small>AINT</small> A<small>UGUSTINE</small>

W<small>HAT</small> I<small>S</small> O<small>UR</small> C<small>OMMON</small> G<small>ROUND</small>?

NANCY

THE SIMPLEST ANSWER to any question is often the most profound. The common ground believers in Jesus Christ have is the level ground at the foot of the cross on which he gave his life for us. It's there, where truth and mercy meet, that we lay down our differing opinions and beliefs. It's there that we all, with uplifted faces, stand amazed by grace.

In 1998 my husband and I were privileged to travel to the Holy Land. It was a life-changing trip for us. One of the most indelible memories we have was the day our band of travelers walked into the Church of St. Anne in Jerusalem. The acoustics in this beautiful Romanesque stone chapel were incredible, and as our tour group filed into some open pews in the back we heard one group and then another singing praise to God in different languages.

At the first opportunity, our worship leader began to lead our group in "Amazing Grace." Our voices had never sounded so pure as they did in that spot on that warm afternoon in Jerusalem. Imagine our surprise when group by group, the other worshippers in the sanctuary began to join in! Whatever their native language, they all seemed to know the English lyrics to this great song of the faith. We were moved to tears. When it was time to leave, one of our pastors turned toward the assemblage, lifted his hands, and boomed out, "We'll see you all in heaven!"

And so we will. There we will be, believers from all nations and persuasions, gathering on the golden streets of the New Jerusalem with all the saints singing, "Holy is the Lamb." It's when we can keep this eternal focus that we are keenly aware of our common ground. For he alone is worthy and worthy of our praise.

This is the common ground on which Alice and I have stood throughout the writing of this book. "For through him we both have access to the Father by one Spirit" (Eph. 2:18). Although Alice and I speak different languages in a sense, it's the common love for Jesus that we see in each other's eyes that first drew us together and continues to keep us close. So it is with all believers, for we see in one another the grace that sustains us, the love that will never die.

I GREW UP in the United Kingdom. The use of the word *kingdom* immediately intimates that there is a sovereign somewhere. Be it a king or a queen, the British Isles, consisting of England, Wales, Northern Ireland, and—the land of my birth—Scotland, are united under a monarch. My parents used to refer to royalty as having "blue blood." When, as a child, I watched bright red blood seep out of my grazed knees after a fall on the school playground, I wondered if the little princesses' cuts bled blue liquid, thus defining them as royalty—or perhaps they did not fall or bleed at all. I saw them as aliens, superior, and other worldly, far beyond a mere mortal such as I. I was a commoner.

I am no longer a commoner for I have been bought by the spilling of royal blood and birthed into the kingdom of heaven by heavenly parentage. For all of us who accept this awesome fact as personal truth, the only thing "common" about us now is a shared life as members of the same royal family—the family of our Father God.

We are family whether we like it or not. In all natural families, siblings and parents are amazingly diverse in personality, persuasion, and passions. However, more often than not, natural families still come home for the holidays despite disagreements, rifts, and sometimes royal fights. Most of the time we still remember one another's birthdays, send the obligatory Mother's and Father's Day cards, though with something less than enthusiasm at times. Though we might wish to disassociate ourselves from obnoxious family members, the unassailable facts are that we are family by birth—by blood—and nothing can change that. Our DNA certifies it.

We are equally bound together in our new creation family by the irrefutable certainty that we are God's children and nothing and no one can change that status. The prince, the pauper, and the prodigal all carry permanent, heavenly DNA (1 Peter 1:23). Still, this new creation, this supernatural family, also labors under the same human limitations and lack of love between its members. Unrenewed minds continue to rule and the royal edicts of King Christ are usurped by the unsurrendered will of his subjects—his children, his kin.

Yet none of our weaknesses and failures can forfeit our status. We often forget that the Christian life is not so much *purpose* driven, as it is *person* driven. Jesus spoke this piercing truth to the most sincerely religious people of his day. "You diligently study the Scriptures because you think that by them you possess eternal life. These are the Scriptures that testify about me, yet you refuse to come to me to have life" (John 5:39–40). He himself is the Life. The word *whole* means "complete, including all aspects, with nothing left out." This word is also the precursor and root of the word *holy*, and that designation is ours because of his imparted holiness. We can do nothing to be holy enough for God's standards: He accomplished and awarded that at Calvary. In fact, because of the completed work of the cross, all humankind is on common ground. Reconciliation has been secured and nothing more is needed in order to bridge the gap between God and humanity. The choice is ours to accept or reject inclusion into the royal family.

Not only do we share royal birth, but also we share common life experiences—hurts, habits, and hang-ups. "We are broken persons and live in broken communities in a state of brokenness," writes Basil Pennington. "We are alienated from ourselves and from each other. We do not readily fit together. We are like a bunch of porcupines trying to huddle together for warmth, who are always driven apart out of fear of the wounds we can inflict upon each other with our quills.... But the ground of our being, our being in God, is totally *common ground* ... then let us drop all the walls and be completely open, and we will find God all in all."[1]

The views and the vistas from the open space of our common ground are limitless when we demolish the retaining walls of dogmas, decrees, or denominations that separate us. Nothing can hinder our living in harmony when we learn to live in dependence upon and in consummate allegiance to the King of Kings and the Lord of Lords. The result is mutual respect when we surrender to his royal rule. The blood that flows through our veins flushes out every particle of selfishness— the selfishness that sabotages our connectedness to one another.

How Do We Become One Despite Our Differences?

ON THE TRIP to Jerusalem I mentioned before, I saw the place where Jesus is said to have knelt in prayer before being arrested. It's a powerful thing to realize that in his hour of greatest need, our Lord chose to pray for his disciples and for us. "Holy Father, protect them by the power of your name—the name you gave me—so that they may be one as we are one," he prayed (John 17:11). We become one because it is the Lord's will for us to be united. Jesus said he came to divide even families, but he was referring to the division between those who believe and those who do not. Within the body of believers, Jesus came to unite, not divide. It is Satan who works to create division in the body of Christ in his fruitless, futile attempts to thwart our unity. We must be on guard, for while Satan has lost the battle, he can still create dissension between believers and within churches, and nothing pleases him more.

What makes it possible for Alice and me to remain friends, even while disagreeing vehemently on the roles of the Christian woman, is that we know we agree on what matters most: that Jesus Christ, the Son of the living God, died for our sins, rose again, and sits on the right hand of God the Father. Our disagreement on some of the less critical issues of the faith, therefore, can't even put a chink in our sisterhood—or our friendship. We know we'll be together in heaven, so we're practicing fellowship now.

Unfortunately, dissension comes naturally to all of us. "The desire to dominate in order to get our own way isn't just confined to marriage," Dee Brestin writes in her book *My Daughter, My Daughter*. "That sad effect of the Fall is the primary cause of strife in all human relationships. It is a warning that we have left the path of God and are following our own way. We have stopped listening. We are beginning to wander in the wilderness—and squabbling all the way. But our heritage, if we go back to the garden before the Fall, was sweet fellowship: with God, and with one another, whether it is our marriage partner or a sister in Christ."[2]

What sustains the unity and fellowship between Alice and me, and between any two believers in conflict, is love: the love of the Father, and the love that we have for one another. Love that is patient, kind, does not envy, does not boast, is not proud, is not rude, is not self-seeking, is not easily angered, keeps no record of wrongs, does not delight in evil but rejoices with the truth! (1 Cor. 13). How could Satan win in the face of such love?

Another thing that sustains us is that we agree to disagree. We don't feel it necessary to hide what we believe in order to protect our friendship, and we haven't fallen into the insidious creeping crud of compromise. How ineffective we would be in this book had we begun by sitting down to negotiate a détente. Imagine my saying, "Oh, OK. I'll give up on headship if you agree to give up on women in the pulpit." It will never happen!

In John's vision of Revelation we see how distasteful wishy-washiness is to God. The letter to the church at Laodicea reads, "So, because you are lukewarm—neither hot nor cold—I am about to spit you out of my mouth" (Rev. 3:16). Jesus, talking to his disciples, said, "Simply let your 'Yes' be 'Yes,' and your 'No,' 'No'; anything beyond this comes from the evil one" (Matt. 5:37). God wants us to take a stand.

A close relative of compromise in today's society is tolerance. By cultural definition, tolerance is no longer the ability to accept one another's differences. Rather, it's the prevailing attitude that there is no absolute truth. That's why Christianity, which is based on immutable truth, is left off the tolerance roster and the diversity bus. Believe anything you want to believe, society says, but don't claim that it's the absolute truth.

Please don't misunderstand. Effective compromise and measured tolerance are both important, but when they're used merely for the sake of unity then they are meaningless and lukewarm. God created us with different personalities and gave us different life experiences. He expects us to have a diversity of opinions and beliefs, and he encourages us to express them. But then, of course, he sent his Son to make sure we would be unified about what matters most.

Throughout the New Testament, believers are urged to encourage one another, rejoice with one another, build one another up, comfort one another, pray for one another, etc. All these "one anothers" together provide a simple outline for how to live the Christian life in community.

NANCY

Our hearts are most united when we pray for one another. It's so true that it's impossible to hate someone for whom you are praying. Praying for one another puts the person we pray for right in front of the throne of God! It allows us to see him or her through God's eyes, and his eyes are the eyes of love. Although we disagree, I've prayed for Alice's writing and she's prayed for mine. We need one another. When we are united and become one, Jesus' prayer is answered.

ALICE

WITHOUT A DOUBT, we *are* one—all the walls of partition have been demolished as far as God is concerned (Eph. 2:11–21). Rather than respecting and delighting in the diversity of the body—as we do with the natural body parts—we insist on cultivating conformity to ensure quality control instead of encouraging radical varietals in the garden of God. He made everything after its own kind and he declared them all good. Science assures us that no two snowflakes are alike—would the same Creator make two people exactly alike? No, of course not, yet that is what religion tries to do. Lord deliver us from cookie-cutter Christianity!

Our differences are decidedly temporal and—in light of eternity—have no lasting power to divide us. Divergent views such as Nancy and I represent in our stands on gender issues are a result of sincere, studied persuasion and have no power to divide us permanently. True, some of the body-at-large hold opinions that appear bizarre, outlandish, and beyond our comprehension. However, even if differences are due to ignorance, immaturity, or pride, we are still family. What sustains our separateness is majoring on minors and minimizing the overarching truth of Christianity—Christ.

I write at a time when there is unparalleled polarization of peoples due to galvanized, lockstep attitudes about any and every issue imaginable. I find it amusing when people assume me to be a registered Republican just because I am a Christian, but their assumption reveals the regrettable truth that Christians are becoming increasingly identified with their opinions more than with their namesake. Jesus tells us that we are to be recognized by our love for one another, not our leanings toward similar political positions on any issue such as right to life, support for war, or preserving the sanctity of marriage. If we demur from the norm in any of these front and center issues, we are in danger of being misunderstood, marginalized, and sometimes ostracized.

While I utterly respect someone's right to march against abortion, for example, I have never felt compelled to do so. When we pressure or expect others to fall in line with our particular conviction or cause, we cause unnecessary division. This world really is not our home and our primary commission is not to clean it up. The Lord Jesus will fold this system up like an old garment so I do not consider investing endless amounts of energy into an entropic system to be the wisest use of my time (Heb. 1:10–12). The

Spirit beckons us to consider the mystery of godliness, not the mastery of the godless—the system and its people. What is this mystery that the ancients longed to see? Nothing less than the staggering new covenant truth—"Christ in you, the hope of glory" (Col. 1:27).

Although most of us are equally familiar with another Bible verse that says something similar, "But he who unites himself with the Lord is one with him in spirit" (1 Cor. 6:17), few of us ponder the repercussion of believing and acting on this seminal truth. This is what would unite us in the here and now; this would influence our words and actions as we, along with the apostle Paul, determine to see no person according to his or her limited human nature, but only after the Spirit. This new kind of seeing would cause us pause when tempted to exclude or harm another in the family. Maybe it was on the road to Damascus that Saul (to become Paul), first had such an epiphany when he heard Jesus say, "Saul, Saul, why do you persecute me? ... I am Jesus, whom you are persecuting" (Acts 9:4–5).

I have an ongoing love affair with the writings of Jeanne Guyon, and so I share her profound observation on our inseparable identity with Christ from her book *Jeanne Guyon Speaks Again*: "In Him we are joined like little drops of water in an ocean! How quickly do the streams join each other and flow together when all the obstacles between us are removed.... Our fellowship is independent of external situations and what other people think. In Christ we cannot be separated from each other, for we are one with Him; and in Him and through Him we are one with each other."[3] Such a revelation—like no other man-made construct of unity—will diminish the differences, eradicate the enmity, and model tolerance and acceptance to a world writhing in conflict, criticism, and confusion.

ALICE

Is There a Place at Jesus' Table for Every Woman?

NANCY

IMAGINE FOR JUST a moment what it would be like to be invited to a dinner party hosted by Jesus. Certainly the long wooden table would be set with the finest white linens and gold flatware. Perhaps flowering wisteria would trail down the center of the table, filling the room with the sweetest of fragrances. Jesus would greet each one of us himself, smiling as he led us gently to the place where our name was engraved on a small white stone. Before the sumptuous feast was served, he would no doubt stoop down by each of our chairs, remove our shoes ... and wash our feet. I can only imagine! The good news is that someday this will be a reality—because, yes, there is a place at the Lord's table for every woman.

No place is more suited for observing the many shapes and sizes of women God created than an exercise class. Part of the success of Curves, the national franchise of women's fitness centers, is that it's for women only. There we are free to show up with "bedhead" and yesterday's makeup—or no makeup at all. It's OK if our bones creak or our shorts are too tight—we're all in it together and we're all accepted just as we are. Isn't that a tiny glimpse of heaven?

I fear too many women are missing out on the fellowship and community that could be theirs at a neighborhood church because they are afraid they don't "fit the mold." The mold may exist only in their imaginations, but they wonder, "Will I fit in and be welcome without a quilted Bible cover with handles, three well-dressed, well-scrubbed children in tow, and a tray of homemade cookies for the welcome booth?" To the extent any of our churches are sending out that kind of message, even inadvertently, we need to stop it!

When Jesus makes out the invitation list for those who will sit with him at his table, there will be one criterion only: Do you believe I am the Son of God who came to take away the sins of the world? Those who say "Yes, Lord, I believe" will receive the invitations. The choices we have made in life won't matter then, for Jesus will redeem and heal the consequences of even our worst choices. He may have something to say to us about how we raised our children, respected our husbands, or loved our neighbors, but none of those things will keep us off the invitation list. Because of his love and grace we can even approach the Communion table and partake of the elements as we remember his sacrifice and receive forgiveness.

I am so incredibly blessed, and humbled, to be loved by women who totally disagree with me

NANCY

about the roles of Christian women. Yet what seems so critically important in the writing of this book may just be a "table topic" at the dinner party Jesus hosts. We'll truly know his heart on all these subjects then, but we won't feel that we are right or wrong—only that we are loved and accepted. I hope Alice will be sitting on one side of me at the table. Won't you take a seat on the other side?

ALICE

WHENEVER OUR EXTENDED family has the increasingly rare bliss of all sitting down at the table together, I always put up name cards at each place setting. This is obviously not because we are unaware of each other's names, but in order that everyone feels that they are chosen and welcome. I have a collection of those place names—written in calligraphy by my husband's hand—from over the years, and they reflect additions as we have grown. They reflect attrition, too, as names of those who are no longer a part of the family disappear. Some of those are now seated at the table of the Lord.

While we look, sometimes more intensely than others, for that future day of feasting at the marriage supper of the Lamb—the day of the consummation of this love affair with our Savior—a table is set in the here and now, too. The only criterion for that setting is that our names first appear in his guest book—the register of those who have accepted the invitation to dine (Rev. 21:27).

Throughout the preceding chapters, we have referred to a wide range of women from various kinds of backgrounds, holding divergent opinions—yet we can find no other qualification for acceptance to God other than in Christ himself. We are all welcome to share in the bounty of his great grace no matter who we are, what we have done, or where we have come from. There is a book in the Bible whose language specializes in articulating God's lavish love; in *The Message*, this reads especially beautifully: "All I want is to sit in his shade, to taste and savor his delicious love. He took me home with him for a festive meal, but his eyes feasted on *me!*" (Song 2:4). That is the wonder of his love. While he loves us corporately—as a body, as a church, as a family—he treats each one of his guests with individual attention as if no one else was at the table.

The table in the here and now is the incredible, life-giving fellowship that we enjoy together. The food that will never run out—and is always on the menu—is love. It satisfies, fills, and makes us forget everything else that separates us as we sit side-by-side under the ravishing gaze of our lover, the King.

Reconciling Our Differences

This is the culmination of our writing together. We are still convinced of the positions we have espoused, but the truth we hold in higher esteem is the oneness we share in Christ and to which all other differences must submit. The Evil One works to divide believers in order to weaken our efforts to proclaim God's plan for salvation. Christ calls us to unity instead.

Epilogue

*When conflict is handled correctly,
we grow closer to each other.*

—Rick Warren

THE GESTATION IS over and the baby is born. I am in awe of how God has directed us over the past months as the seeds—the thoughts of our inmost beings—have formed into the fully fledged book you now hold in your hands. The process of writing never fails to amaze me. How many mornings have I started out staring at a blank screen, only to have, by day's end, more words and thoughts on the topic than required.

In the articulating of my convictions, I have become more convinced than ever of the mutuality of women and men in God's plan. I am more fully persuaded that submission is an imperative—equally vital for both female and male: first to their

ALICE

God and then to one another. Unbent wills wreak havoc in homes, and selfish, unsubmissive hearts cripple every relationship. I have melted afresh under the gaze of the Father's love as I presented his awesome heart to you. And I—known to be opinionated and sometimes stroppy—have grown in gentleness as I've worked with my wonderful coauthor. Nancy is the epitome of integrity, kindness, and grace. I love and cherish her expression of Christ.

Although we wrote and compiled our answers independently of each other during the creative process, occasionally we have surrendered our material to the scrutiny of the other for clarification and perspective. On one such occasion Nancy requested that I read and evaluate one of her chapters to determine if what she had written made sense. I responded, "Yes, it's very well-written—and makes me as mad as ever." We do not agree—that's the point of the book. Many have commented to me, on hearing of the hope for this collaboration, "If you can inspire folks to respect one another despite their differences, you will have written a very special kind of book."

In presenting differing views on issues we each consider very important to the smooth and healthy functioning of our heavenly family on earth, we know that they will be valuable to the reader only to the extent that we have respected one another's firmly held opinions. To have done otherwise would simply read and resonate as sounding brass or tinkling cymbals—empty of love. We have tried to model reciprocal respect for

ALICE

individual choices no matter how much they differ from our own. That is our intention in having you, the reader, consider the questions in the readers' guide at the end of this book. If we have stirred you to think—to make God-directed choices for yourself—then we have achieved our goal. If you feel loved no matter what you choose to believe—we have scored substantial bonus points.

It is my hope that Jesus has emerged as preeminent. I echo the words of the unsurpassed purveyor of principles, Richard Wurmbrand, in commenting on his many written reflections and ruminations while in solitary confinement in a communist jail. He wrote in *Sermons in Solitary Confinement*, "These sermons are not to be judged for their dogmatic content. I did not live on dogma then. Nobody can. The soul feeds on Christ, not on teachings about him."[1]

NANCY

AS SO OFTEN happens in the life women share, it all began over lunch. Alice and I carved out some time for a leisurely meal at one of our favorite restaurants and simply savored one another's presence. Soon the Spirit began to give us a spirit of unity. More lunches followed, and although we discovered our disagreements on the roles of the Christian woman were even stronger than we initially suspected, so was our commitment to each other. Soon this book began to take shape. We knew without a doubt that the Lord wanted us to find a way to write it together in order to honor the passion he had given us, the friendship he had given us—and the unity that brings him glory.

We were aware we took on some risk with this assignment: risk that our friendship would suffer. Instead, it grew stronger. We learned that venturing deeper into friendship with someone who doesn't exactly agree with everything we hold to be true is rejuvenating, growth-inducing, and just plain fun when we, as women, have maturity and confidence in who we are through Jesus Christ.

We began this book by writing our spiritual journeys. The thing about a spiritual journey is that it continues until the day we die. My younger son, Tim, is a Presbyterian pastor and chaplain in the Army Reserve. As I write this, he may soon be going to Iraq. If so, God will be giving me new opportunities to trust in him and to deepen my faith. But because the writing of this book has also been an amazing spiritual experience for me, and taken me much farther on the journey than I ever imagined, it's important to tell you the rest of the story.

Like most journeys, this one had its pitfalls, but it also had its humor. During one work session at my house I went out to get the mail and was horrified to see that Alice's car, parked prodigiously in my driveway, bore the bumper sticker: Equality is biblical.

Later that same afternoon, when it was time for her to leave, her car wouldn't start. My years as a single mom gave me some expertise, and my plan of action included finding the jumper cables in the garage or giving Alice a push down the hill so she could pop the clutch. What she chose to do was call her husband and say, "I don't know. It just won't start! What should I do?" Immediately we realized how "un-stereotypical" our responses were given our stands on the roles of Christian women. We dissolved into laughter, went inside, and enjoyed a cool drink until both her Jim and mine arrived on the scene to assess the situation.

I began writing this book with the firm belief that I was right and Alice was wrong. I thought that perhaps misguided women of her persuasion would pick up the book and, maybe out of boredom or curiosity, read my answers to the questions as well. Then I would have a chance to persuade them to join the winning team of complementarian women. (I wonder if complementarian will fit on a T-shirt?)

I haven't changed any of my strongly held positions on biblical womanhood during the writing process, but the Lord used a deeper look into Alice's kind and generous heart to show me that unity with a fellow believer is far more important than being right. Just as he told me that it wasn't my job to worry about my stepdaughter Joelle's decision to go into church leadership, he told me that Alice was accountable to him. I pray that even those who disagree with me will be able to glean something from what I've written to enrich their lives, but I know that all God expected me to do was to write down what he put on my heart.

NANCY

To the extent that I have been able to do that, I give him the credit and the glory.

In a letter to the church in Rome, Paul writes, "May the God who gives endurance and encouragement give you a spirit of unity among yourselves as you follow Christ Jesus, so that with one heart and mouth you may glorify the God and Father of our Lord Jesus Christ" (Rom. 15:5–6). And all the people said—Amen!

Readers' Guide

For Personal Reflection or Group Study

CHAPTER 1
WONDERING WHO WE ARE: THE ESSENTIAL WOMAN

1. How would you describe your own essential identity?

2. How are male and female roles defined in your family? Who does what and why?

3. Do you feel you embody all the roles God designed for women? Why or why not?

Chapter 2
Saying I Do: The Design of a Wife

1. If you are married, what three words or phrases best describe you as a wife?

2. Do you believe that changing the way you view marriage could change your husband (or potential husband) as well?

3. What would mutual submission look like in your marriage? What does Galatians 3:28 mean to you?

Chapter 3
Giving for a Lifetime: Motherhood

1. Is motherhood always a natural choice? Is this true for you? Explain.

Readers' Guide

2. If you're a mother, how fulfilling is motherhood for you? What makes it such a coveted goal in a woman's life?

3. What is a mother's role in developing her children's respect for their father?

Chapter 4
Finding Our Niche: The Working Woman

1. Consider what satisfying work means to you. Explain.

2. What price are you or your family paying for the choices you've made about work? Is it time to reevaluate?

3. What are the expectations you've place on yourself regarding work? Where do you think these came from?

Chapter 5
Following Our Calling: The Ministry of a Woman

1. With what constraints are you familiar in the pursuit of the call of God on your life?

2. What argument is used to validate women in leadership?

3. What does it mean to lead through influence? How have you seen that kind of leadership exhibited?

Chapter 6
Confronting Hard Questions: Challenging Issues

1. Before reading this, were you familiar with the concept of "male covering"? How do your single friends feel about it?

2. Is homosexuality the worst sin? How do you respond when you encounter a gay Christian?

3. Our choices often have consequences. What long-term ramifications exist in your life because of choices you've made in the past?

Chapter 7
Leaving Our Hearts Behind: A Lasting Legacy

1. Have you been mentored by an older woman? What kind of modeling did you see?

2. What is the legacy you want to leave as a woman?

3. What could you share about your life that would comfort or guide other women?

Chapter 8
Loving One Another Anyway: Unity in Christ

1. Is unity a priority in your relationships? In your estimation, what is the biggest obstacle to living in harmony in the body of Christ?

2. What is God's view of unity? Why is it so important to him?

3. Now that you've read this book, complete the experience by writing what you think God has told you about your role as a Christian woman and the blessedness of unity in him.

Notes

CHAPTER 1
WONDERING WHO WE ARE: THE ESSENTIAL WOMAN

1. La Donna Osborn, "Redemption: An Image of Biblical Equality," *Priscilla Papers* 13, no. 3 (Summer 1999): 5.
2. Alvin John Schmidt, *Veiled and Silenced* (Macon, GA: Mercer University Press, 1990), 21.
3. Ibid., 42.
4. Larry Crabb, *Men and Women, Enjoying the Difference* (Grand Rapids: Zondervan, 1993), 133.
5. Ibid., 143.
6. John Gray, *Men Are from Mars, Women Are from Venus* (New York: HarperCollins Publishers, 1992), 10.
7. Ray McClendon, *Dr. Laura: A Mother in America* (Colorado Springs: Chariot Victor Publishing, 1999), 106.
8. Anna Quindlen, "We're Missing Some Senators," *Newsweek* (March 21, 2005): 70.
9. Carolyn Custis James, *When Life and Beliefs Collide* (Grand Rapids: Zondervan, 2001), 171.
10. Gilbert Bilezikian, "A Challenge," *Priscilla Papers* 15, no. 4 (Fall 2001): 8.

CHAPTER 2
SAYING I DO: THE DESIGN OF A WIFE

1. K. T. Oslin, *Songs from an Aging Sex Bomb: 80's Ladies* (New York: BMG Music, 1993).
2. Rebecca Mead, "Conditional Surrender," *The New Yorker* (April 2001): 82.
3. Gretchen Gaebelein Hull, "Jesus and Family Values," *Priscilla Papers* 15, no. 2 (Spring 2001): 17.
4. Oswald Chambers, *My Utmost for His Highest* (Westwood, NJ: Barbour and Company, Inc., 1935), 297.

5. Judson W. VanDeVenter, "I Surrender All," *The Hymnal* (Nashville: Word Music, 1986), 366.
6. P. B. "Bunny" Wilson, *Liberated Through Submission* (Eugene, OR: Harvest House Publishers, 1997), 15.
7. Stormie Omartian, *The Power of a Praying Wife* (Eugene, OR: Harvest House Publishers, 1997), 35.
8. Susan Hunt, *By Design* (Wheaton, IL: Crossway Books, 1994), 34.
9. Wilson, *Liberated Through Submission*, 191.
10. Jeff VanVonderen, *Families Where Grace Is in Place* (Minneapolis: Bethany House Publishers, 1992), 86.
11. Alexander Strauch, *Men and Women, Equal Yet Different* (Colorado Springs: Lewis and Roth Publishers, 1999), 55.
12. Ibid., 55–56.
13. Gilbert Bilezikian, "The Issue I Can't Evade," *Priscilla Papers* 17, no. 2 (Spring 2003): 5.
14. Ibid.
15. Kevin Giles, *The Trinity and Subordinationism* (Downers Grove, IL: InterVarsity Press, 2002), 115.

Chapter 3
Giving for a Lifetime: Motherhood

1. Alice Miller, *The Drama of the Gifted Child* (New York: Basic Books, 1997), 42–43.
2. Sarah Blaffer Hrdy, *Mother Nature* (New York: Ballantine, 1999), 26.
3. Betty Rollin, "Baby Blues," *AARP Magazine* (July & August 2003): 37–38.
4. Richard and Catherine Kroeger, *I Suffer Not a Woman* (Grand Rapids: Baker Books, 1992), 177.
5. Michelle Lovric, *Mothers* (Philadelphia: Courage Books, 1993), 9.
6. Anna Quindlen, "The Up Side," *Guideposts Magazine* (September 2002): 10.
7. Dotson Rader, "She Made Her Dreams Come True," *Parade Magazine* (June 15, 2003): 5.
8. Judy Goldman, *Early Leaving* (New York: William Morrow, 2004), 264.
9. Gigi Schweikert, *There's a Perfect Little Angel in Every Child* (West Monroe, LA: Howard Publishing, 2005), 1.
10. Judith Warner, "Mommy Madness," *Newsweek* (February 21, 2005).

Chapter 4
Finding Our Niche: The Working Woman

1. Rhoda Thomas Tripp, *The International Thesaurus of Quotations* (New York: Penguin Books, 1970), 706.
2. Rick Warren, *The Purpose-Driven Life* (Grand Rapids: Zondervan, 2002), 227.
3. J. Lee Grady, *Ten Lies the Church Tells Women* (Lake Mary, FL: Charisma House, 2000), 158.
4. Carol Penner, *Women and Men: Gender in the Church* (Scottsdale, PA: Herald Press, 1998), 46.
5. Dorothy Patterson, "The High Calling of Wife and Mother in Biblical Perspective," *Recovering Biblical Manhood and Womanhood: A Response to Evangelical Feminism*, ed. John Piper and Wayne Grudem

(Wheaton, IL: Crossway Books, 1991), 365.
6. Lisa Belkin, quoted in Joel Belz, "A Powerful Force," *World* (November 8, 2003): 4.
7. Claudia Wallis, "The Case for Staying Home," *Time* (March 22, 2004): 53.
8. Grady, 157.
9. Ruth Haley Barton, *Equal to the Task* (Downers Grove, IL: InterVarsity Press, 1998), 133.
10. Helen Clark and Elizabeth Carnegie, *She Was Aye Workin'* (Oxford, England: White Cockade Publishing, 2003), 11–12.
11. Dave Eberhart, "Women in Combat," *NewsMax* (February 2005): 22.
12. Warren, 255.

Chapter 5
Following Our Calling: The Ministry of a Woman

1. Christiane Carlson-Theis, "Hermeneutics in Pink and Blue," *Priscilla Papers* 16, no. 4 (Fall 2002): 5.
2. Martin Smith, "Shout to the North" (Curious? Music UK, 1995).
3. Susan Hunt and Peggy Hutcheson, *Leadership for Women in the Church* (Grand Rapids: Zondervan, 1991), 40.
4. Bonnidell Clouse and Robert G. Clouse, editors, *Women in Ministry: Four Views* (Downers Grove, IL: InterVarsity Press, 1989), 46.
5. Kirk Dearman, "We Bring the Sacrifice of Praise" (Franklin, TN: John T. Benson Publishing Company, 1984).
6. James R. Payton Jr., "A Tale of Two Cultures," *Priscilla Papers* 16, no. 1 (Winter 2002).

Chapter 6
Confronting Hard Questions: Challenging Issues

1. Mary A. Kassian, *The Feminist Gospel: The Movement to Unite Feminism with the Church* (Wheaton, IL: Crossway Books, 1992), 58.
2. The Council on Biblical Manhood and Womanhood, http://www.cbmw.org/questions/41.php.
3. Diane Passno, *Feminism: Mystique or Mistake?* (Wheaton, IL: Tyndale House Publishers, 2000), 176.
4. Rebecca Merrill Groothuis, "Sexuality, Spirituality, and Feminist Religion," www.cbeinternational.org/new/free_articles/sexuality_spirituality.shtml.
5. Paul R. Smith, *Is It Okay to Call God "Mother"?* (Peabody, MA: Hendrickson Publishers, 1993), 147.
6. Charles Swindoll, *Strike the Original Match* (Wheaton, IL: Tyndale House Publishers, 1990), 135.
7. T. D. Jakes, *The Lady, Her Lover, and Her Lord* (New York: The Berkeley Publishing Group, 2000), 190–191.
8. Source obtained from the Internet: Malcolm Smith, "If Only," www.malcolmsmith.org/home.asp, 2005.
9. Lauren Winner, "Singleminded," *World* (July 3/10, 2004): 45.
10. Elisabeth Elliot, "Virginity," *Elisabeth Elliot Newsletter* (March/April 1990): 2–3.

11. Gerald G. May, M.D., *The Dark Night of the Soul* (New York: HarperCollins, 2004), 22.
12. http://ww2.intouch.org/site/c.7nKFISNvEqG/b.1034907/k.8A72/Henrietta_Mears.htm.
13. Condoleezza Rice, 2005. Interview on *Fox News Channel*, quoted in *US News and World Report* (May 2, 2005).
14. Where Grace Abounds, "Our Approach," http://www.wheregraceabounds.org/philosophy.html.
15. "Homosexuality: An Interview with Jesus" by Rowland Croucher, http://jmm.aaa.net/au/articles/12135.htm.

Chapter 7
Leaving Our Hearts Behind: A Lasting Legacy

1. Sarah Ban Breathnach, *Something More, Excavating Your Authentic Self* (New York: Warner Books, 1998), 175.
2. Cynthia Heald, *Becoming a Woman of Freedom* (Colorado Springs: NavPress, 1992), 99.
3. Julian of Norwich, *Enfolded in Love* (London, England: Darton Longman & Todd Ltd., 1980), 33.
4. Susan Hunt and Barbara Thompson, *The Legacy of Biblical Womanhood* (Wheaton, IL: Crossway Books, 2003), 88.
5. Ibid., 76.
6. Ibid., 78.
7. Susan Hunt, *Spiritual Mothering* (Wheaton, IL: Crossway Books, 1992), 45.
8. Julian of Norwich, 17.
9. Anne Seagraves, *High-Spirited Women of the West* (Hayden, ID: Wesanne Publications, 1992), 41.
10. Charles Wesley, "Jesus, Lover of My Soul," *The Scottish Psalter* (London, England: Oxford University Press, 1929), 473.
11. Danielle Crittenden, *What Our Mothers Didn't Tell Us* (New York: Simon & Schuster, 1999), 73.
12. Barbara Mouser, *Five Aspects of Woman* (Waxahachie, TX: ICGS, 1995), 3.18.
13. Amy Stephens, "Why God Says Wait," *Focus on the Family Magazine* (February 2005, 19).
14. Justice Rebecca Love Kourlis, "The Feminine in Feminism," February 28, 2003, http://www.womenof.com/articles/ai020298.asp.

Chapter 8
Loving One Another Anyway: Unity in Christ

1. Basil Pennington, "Common Ground," *Union Life* 22, no. 6 (November/December 1997): 9.
2. Dee Brestin, *My Daughter, My Daughter* (Colorado Springs: Cook Communications, 1999), 70.
3. Jeanne Guyon, *Jeanne Guyon Speaks Again* (Auburn, ME: Seedsowers, 1989), 79–80. Note: some editions are titled *Intimacy with Christ*.

Epilogue

1. Richard Wurmbrand, *Sermons in Solitary Confinement* (London, England: Hodder and Stoughton Ltd., 1969), 7.

Recommended Reading List

Of all the books and articles we read to research issues in this book, a few stand out as the most informative. Here are our favorite sources to get you started on further study.

ALICE RECOMMENDS ...

Barton, Ruth Haley. *Equal to the Task, Men and Women in Partnership.* Downers Grove, IL: InterVarsity Press, 1998.

Bibb, Stephanie F. *Women's Liberation: Jesus Style, Messages of Spirituality and Wisdom for Today's Woman.* Lansing, IL: Ruach Communications, Inc., 1998.

Bilezikian, Gilbert. *Beyond Sex Roles, What the Bible Says About a Woman's Place in Church and Family.* Grand Rapids: Baker Books, 1985.

Bristow, John Temple. *What Paul Really Said About Women: An Apostle's Liberating Views on Equality in Marriage, Leadership, and Love.* New York: HarperCollins, 1988.

Giles, Kevin. *The Trinity and Subordinationism.* Downers Grove, IL: InterVarsity Press, 2002.

Grady, J. Lee. *Ten Lies the Church Tells Women.* Lake Mary, FL: Charisma House, 2000.

Grenz, Stanley J., and Denise Muir Kjesbo. *Women in the Church: A Biblical Theology of Women in Ministry*. Downers Grove, IL: InterVarsity Press, 1995.

Groothuis, Rebecca Merrill. *Good News for Women: A Biblical Picture of Gender Equality*. Grand Rapids: Baker Books, 1997.

James, Carolyn Custis. *When Life and Beliefs Collide*. Grand Rapids: Zondervan, 2001.

Keener, Craig S. *Paul, Women and Wives: Marriage and Women's Ministry in the Letters of Paul*. Peabody, MA: Hendrickson Publishers, Inc, 1992.

Kroeger, Richard Clark, and Catherine Clark Kroeger. *I Suffer Not a Woman*. Grand Rapids: Baker Books, 1992.

Penner, Carol. *Women and Men: Gender in the Church*. Scottsdale, PA: Herald Press, 1998.

Schmidt, Alvin John. *Veiled and Silenced: How Culture Shaped Sexist Theory*. Macon, GA: Mercer University Press, 1990.

Smith, Paul R. *Is It Okay to Call God Mother?* Peabody, MA: Hendrickson Publishers, 1993.

Nancy Recommends ...

Brestin Dee, with Lori Beckler. *My Daughter, My Daughter*. Colorado Springs: Chariot Victor Publishing, 1999.

Crabb, Larry. *Men and Women, Enjoying the Difference*. Grand Rapids: Zondervan, 1993.

Crittenden, Danielle. *What Our Mothers Didn't Tell Us*. New York: Simon & Schuster, 1999.

DeMoss, Nancy Leigh. *Lies Women Believe and the Truth That Sets Them Free*. Chicago: Moody Press, 2001.

Eldredge, John and Stasi. *Captivating*. Nashville: Thomas Nelson, Inc., 2005.

Farrar, Mary. *Choices*. Sisters, OR: Multnomah Books, 1994.

Hunt, Susan. *By Design*. Wheaton, IL: Crossway Books, 1994.

Hunt, Susan, and Peggy Hutcheson. *Leadership for Women in the Church*. Grand Rapids: Zondervan, 1991.

Hunt, Susan, and Barbara Thompson. *The Legacy of Biblical Womanhood*. Wheaton, IL: Crossway Books, 2003.

Mouser, Barbara K. *Five Aspects of Woman*. Waxahachie, TX: International Council for Gender Studies, 1995.
Passno, Diane. *Feminism: Mystique or Mistake?* Wheaton, IL: Tyndale House, 2000.
Piper, John, and Wayne Grudem. *Recovering Biblical Manhood and Womanhood: A Response to Evangelical Feminism.* Wheaton, IL: Crossway Books, 1991.
Strauch, Alexander. *Men and Women: Equal Yet Different.* Colorado Springs: Lewis & Roth Publishers, 1999.
Wilson, P. B. "Bunny." *Liberated Through Submission.* Eugene, OR: Harvest House Publishers, 1997.

Other Books Presenting Both Sides of the Issues Include:

Blomberg, Craig, Thomas R. Schreiner, James R. Beck, and Ann L. Bowman. *Two Views on Women and Ministry*. Grand Rapids: Zondervan, 2001.
Clouse, Bonnidell, and Robert G. Clouse, eds. *Women in Ministry: Four Views*. Downers Grove, IL: InterVarsity Press, 1989.

About Nancy

NANCY PARKER BRUMMETT is a freelance writer, author, and speaker living in Colorado Springs, CO. Her previous books include *Simply the Savior* (Cook), *It Takes a Home* (Cook), and *The Journey of Elisa* (Cook). A conversational style and genuine concern for women are the hallmarks of Nancy's writing and speaking ministries. A former single mom and now a wife, mother, stepmother, and grandmother, she writes and speaks from her heart and inspires readers and audiences to respond with theirs. Nancy and her husband Jim have four married children and ten grandchildren in their blended family. She can be contacted at grancycomm@msn.com.

About Alice

ALICE SCOTT-FERGUSON was born in Scotland and immigrated to the USA with her husband and three children over thirty years ago. She currently lives in Phoenix, AZ. She is a life-long champion for women to be all that they were created to be in Christ. That passion is evident in both her speaking and writing. She has authored two other books—*Little Women, Big God* (Essence) and *Mothers Can't Be Everywhere, But God Is* (Cladach)—and has written innumerable articles. She continues to create a variety of Bible studies and teaches many of them in her local church. Her family has now expanded to include six grandchildren. Alice can be contacted at Free2b@qwest.net.

Additional copies of RECONCILABLE DIFFERENCES
and other Life Journey titles are available
wherever good books are sold.

If you have enjoyed this book,
or if it has had an impact on your life,
we would like to hear from you.

Please contact us at:

LIFE JOURNEY BOOKS
Cook Communications Ministries, Dept. 201
4050 Lee Vance View
Colorado Springs, CO 80918

Or visit our Web site:
www.cookministries.com

LIFE JOURNEY®
Bringing Home the Message for Life